DRAGONS, CRYSTALS & CHAINMAILLE

Jewelry Designs to Inspire Your Imagination

JANE DANLEY CRUZ

KALMBACH BOOKS

WAUKESHA, WI

Kalmbach Books
21027 Crossroads Circle
Waukesha, Wisconsin 53186
www.JewelryAndBeadingStore.com

Published in 2017
21 20 19 18 17   1 2 3 4 5

Manufactured in the United States of America

ISBN: 978-1-62700-400-8
EISBN: 978-1-62700-401-5

Editor: Dianne Wheeler
Book Design: Lisa Bergman
Technical Editor: Dana Meredith
Proofreader: Annie Pennington
Photographer: William Zuback

Library of Congress Control Number: 2016943707

Table of Contents

Introduction 4
Basics 103
Acknowledgments 111
About the Author 111

Brooches and Accessories

Eye of the Dragon ring.............................. 6

Hammered Scroll pin 8

Maid Marion tiara 12

Royal Potions pendant 16

Lady of the Lake armlet............................ 19

Vassel's brooch 22

Necklaces

Prisoner's Chain necklace.......................... 28

The Chieftan choker 30

Ancient Dragonfly necklace....................... 33

Tangled Roots choker................................ 36

Stonehenge necklace................................. 40

Mystic Crystal necklace 43

Magic Ring lariat 46

Claw and Crystal Torque necklace............ 49

Fortune Teller's necklace 52

Bracelets

Forever Entwined cuff................................. 56

Mystic Warrior cuff 59

Dragon's Claws bracelet 62

Stolen Dreams bracelet 65

Corset cuff 68

Blacksmith's forged bracelet...................... 71

The Tribal Queen's Gauntlet bracelet 74

Hobnail wrist wrap 78

Earrings

Trembling Scales earrings........................... 82

Orb of the Raven earrings 84

Lady-in-Waiting earrings 86

Amethyst Alchemy earrings 89

Dragon's Gold earrings............................... 92

Serpent's Scales earrings............................ 94

Tethys earrings.. 96

Chainmaille Bellflower earrings 100

I've had a love affair
with jewelry for as long
as I can remember.

Introduction

I remember those special occasions as a small child when my mother would get out her black lacquered jewelry box and let us examine the beautiful jewelry that had been handed down to her. Holding those treasures in my hand, I would fantasize about the men and women who had once worn this jewelry, what their lives must have been like, and what meaning these precious bits of gold and gems may have had for them.

As I grew older, my taste in jewelry grew bolder. In college I joined a group of Madrigal singers; although I wasn't overly fond of the theatrics or the music, I was fascinated by the historical era. However, of most importance was the fact that the rich brocade and velvet costumes provided the perfect canvas for my medieval costume jewelry collection.

Today, it's so exciting to see fashion magazines splashing medieval- and fantasy-themed jewelry across their glossy pages. It's truly an era of inspired imagination. Dragons have stormed onto runways, best-selling books, movies, and television series. It's in vogue to adorn oneself with crosses, swords, Celtic symbols,

and heavy chain. Exclusive fashion and jewelry designers are incorporating spikes, leather, natural crystals, and hammered metal into their high-priced designs — and you can too!

Most of the projects in this book use tools and materials you can find at your local craft and hobby store. I used a wide variety of techniques like wirework, basic stitching, simple chainmaille, and kumihimo so you're sure to find something you like. Where possible, I used tools you already have, like your fingers or a pencil, but occasionally you may need to purchase specific supplies. Explore your own cache of jewelry findings and craft supplies as well as the aisles of your favorite craft or hobby shop.

I hope the jewelry and techniques in this book will inspire you to create your own fantasy and medieval jewelry.

Jane Danley

Brooches and Accessories

Eye of the Dragon ring

An amulet may protect you from the fiery
gaze of the dragon. Beware — should it turn,
fire will rain down upon you.

Instructions

1. On a comfortable length of Fireline, string 40 11º cylinder beads, leaving a 4" tail. Tie the beads into a ring with square knots **(Basics, p. 110)**. Sew through all

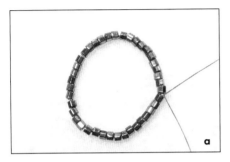

a

of the beads three or four more times to secure them **(a)**. Cut the tail and the working thread close to the bead work.
2. Apply a thin layer of E6000 inside the bezel blank and on the back of the cabochon **(b)**.
3. Center the cabochon in the bezel, making sure the iris of the eye is perpendicular to the ring band. Press firmly **(c)**.
4. Slide the ring of beads over the cabochon and, using your fingers or a toothpick, push the ring firmly down into the glue **(d)**.
5. Clean up any seepage with a toothpick.

MATERIALS & TOOLS

- **40 11º hex cylinder beads, metallic luster forest green**
- 14mm reptile eye cabochon
- 18mm round bezel ring blank
- Fireline 6-lb. test

- Beading needle #10
- E6000 glue
- Scissors
- Toothpick *(optional)*

b

c

d

designer NOTE

If rings are not your thing, make a pendant using the same technique. Just adjust the number of cylinder beads to fit the size of the cabochon and bezel pendant blank. If the cabochon is smaller, try adding two rows of beads around the outer edge.

Hammered Scroll pin

The night's dark mist splashes across your face as you charge to the castle. Keep your father's pin tight to your cloak; remember, his final commands must be honored.

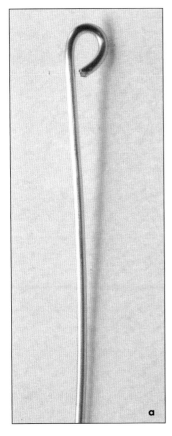

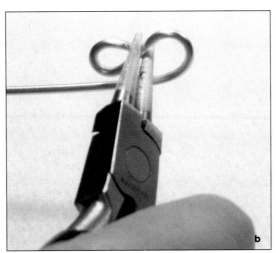

- 11" 12-gauge Artistic wire, silver
- 13" 12-gauge Artistic wire, silver

- Bench block
- Chasing hammer
- Metal file
- Roundnose pliers

Instructions

Ring

1. Using roundnose pliers and a 13" piece of wire, make an 8mm plain loop **(Basics, p. 108) (a)**.

2. Position the pliers at the base of the plain loop and bend the wire back over the pliers in the opposite direction, making a larger loop **(b)**.

3. Using your fingers, continue to gently bend the wire around the bottom of the plain loop and back up towards the top **(c)**.

4. Work as in steps 1–3 on the other end of the wire, mirroring the bends **(d)**.

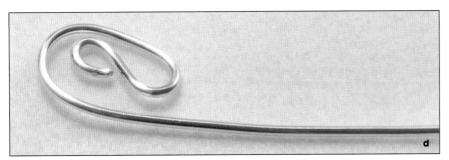

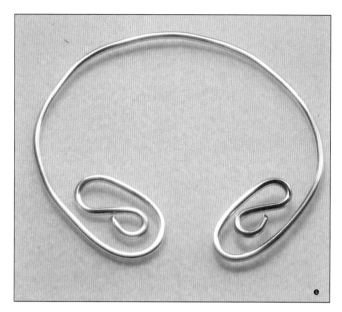

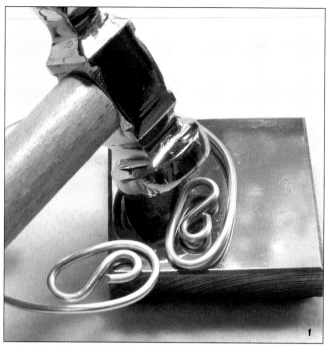

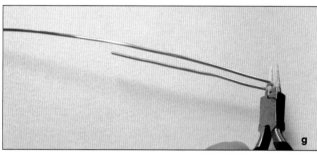

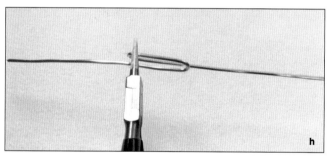

5. Continue to gently form the wire into a circle with the loops toward the inside **(e)**.

6. Place the circle onto the bench block and gently hammer it with the flat face of a chasing hammer **(f)**.

Stick pin

1. Position the roundnose pliers approximately 3½" from one end of the 11" piece of wire and bend the wire 180 degrees **(g)**.

2. Position the pliers 1" from the previous bend. Make a second 180-degree bend, down and back towards the first bend created in step 1 **(h)**.

3. Position the pliers in the first bend created, and make another 180-degree bend up and back **(i)**.

4. Position the pliers near the bend created in step 2, and bend the wire to the side and back along itself **(j)**.

5. Position the pliers where the wire meets itself, and make another bend to the side **(k)**.

6. Positon the pliers at the end of the wire, and coil the wire back on itself until it meets the side bend created in step 5.

7. Using the chasing hammer and the bench block, hammer the stick.

8. File the straight end of the stick into a rounded point with a metal file **(l)**.

9. Thread the pin onto the circle **(m)**. From this point on, you will work the pin as it is wrapped around the circle.

10. Use your fingers to manipulate the coils and bends to a pleasing design.

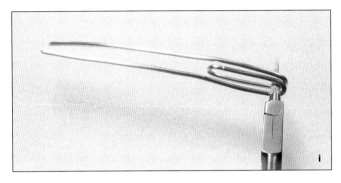

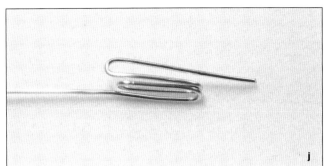

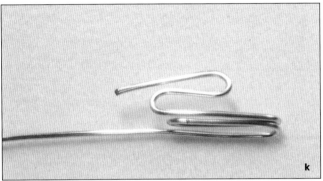

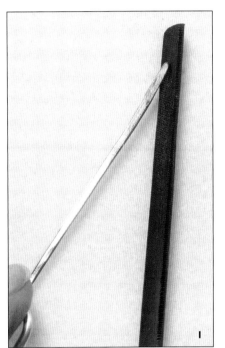

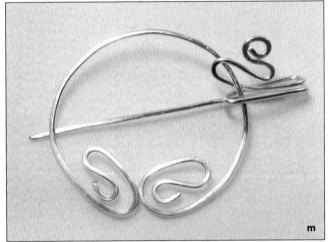

TIP If you open the bends and coils, you can secure the decorative end of the stick to the circle **(n)** in order to keep it in position once you have inserted it through your material.

Maid Marion tiara

While only a queen may wear a crown, many a fair maiden will decorate her hair with jeweled bands and ribbons. Perhaps Robin Hood stole this tiara.

- 3g 8º seed beads, color A
- 3g 8º seed beads, color B
- 1g 8º seed beads, color C
- 1g 11º seed beads, color D
- 4mm plain, gold-colored wire tiara frame
- **6** 8mm bicone crystals, red
- Fireline 6-lb. test

∽

- Beading needle #10
- Scissors

a

b

c

Instructions

Woven band

1. On 3' of Fireline, pick up three color A 8º seed beads, three color B 8º seed beads, three As, and three Bs **(a)**. Tie the beads into a ring with a square knot **(Basics, p. 110)**, leaving a 6" tail **(b)**. This creates the first unit. Continue through the first six beads to exit the third B **(c)**.

2. Pick up three Bs, three As, and three Bs, and sew through the first three Bs added in the previous step **(d)**. Your thread is exiting the same B it exited at the start of this step. This creates the second unit.

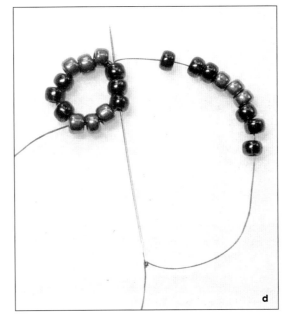

d

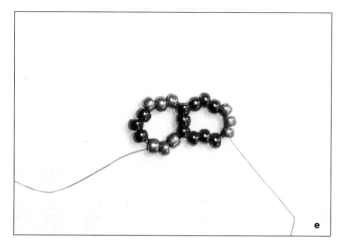

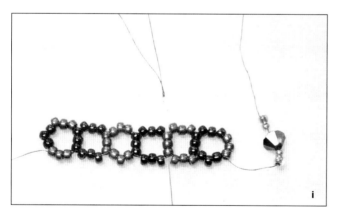

3. Continue through the first six beads added in this step **(e)**. You are now in position to begin the next unit.

4. Pick up three As, three Bs, and three As, and sew through the three As added in the previous step **(f)**. This completes the third unit. Continue through the first six beads added in this step **(g)**. You are now in position to begin the next unit.

5. Work as in steps 2 and 3 until you have completed 47 units. End the threads **(Basics, p. 110)**.

TIP Photos i – l demonstrate the remaining steps on a small swatch that is not threaded onto the headband to make it easier to see the beadwork. However, I have found working with the beadwork on the headband is actually easier.

k

l

Assembly and embellishment

1. Thread the beadwork onto the head-band by weaving the headband under and over the vertical rows of beads **(h)**.

2. Identify the center unit in the bead-work. Add 18" of Fireline to the beadwork **(Basics, p. 110)**.

3. Notice that each unit has four "walls." Each wall is made up of three As or three Bs. Sew through the beadwork so your thread is exiting the last bead in a vertical wall of the center unit.

4. Pick up a color C 8° seed bead, a color D 11° seed bead, an 8mm bicone crystal, a D, and a C. Skip the opposite vertical wall of the center unit. This will be on the back of your headband if you have threaded your beadwork onto the metal headband. Sew through the three beads in the next vertical wall **(i)** making sure the beads just added cross the band in a diagonal direction. Snug up the beads **(j)**.

5. Pick up a C and a D, and sew through the crystal added in the previous step **(k)**. Pick up a D and a C, and sew through the three beads in the same vertical wall of the center unit in step 3 **(l)**.

m

6. Retrace the threadpaths as in steps 4 and 5 to secure the crystal.

7. Work as in steps 4, 5, and 6 on one side of the center unit and then sew through the beadwork and repeat on the other side of the center unit to embellish the top of the headband for a total of six crystal embellishments **(m)**. End the threads.

Royal Potions pendant

Rodent bones, glitter from the stars, and the tears of a widowed maiden make up the Queen's sleeping potion. Will it be nightmares again tonight?

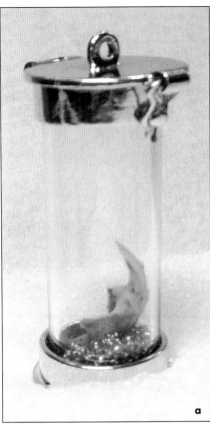

a

Instructions

1. Make a depression in the styrofoam block by pushing the bottle locket down into the foam. Pour a small amount of seed beads into the bottom of the locket. Add a few rodent bones. Set the locket into the depression **(a)**.

2. Mix the jewelry resin according to the manufacturer's instructions.

3. Pour enough resin into the locket to fill it approximately ⅓ of the way up **(b)**.

MATERIALS & TOOLS

- Several 15º seed beads
- **2** or **3** 3mm crystals
- **1** or **2** small charms
- Rodent bones (from owl pellets)
- Glitter in several colors
- ¾" x 1½" small glass bottle locket
- Jewelry resin
- Styrofoam block

b

c

d

4. Pour a small amount of one color of glitter into the locket **(c)**.

5. Pour a small amount of resin in **(d)**, then add another color of glitter. Keep adding layers of resin, glitter, resin, glitter until you have filled the locket **(e)**. Set aside to dry.

6. After about an hour, you can add small charms, crystals, or more glitter before the resin has hardened. They will sink down slightly into the resin, drawing some of the glitter with them for a galaxy effect.

7. Attach silk cords or a chain to the bottle locket.

e

Lady of the Lake armlet

Legend leads many a wanderer to the shores of the misty lake in search of Excalibur. The spirit of Camelot lives on—and the lady waits still for the next worthy king.

- 28–32" 12-gauge Artistic wire, silver
- 12" 20-gauge Artistic wire, silver
- Fairy tale sword charm with jump ring

- Chainnose pliers
- Flatnose pliers
- Sharpie marker
- Wire cutters

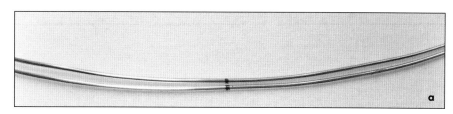

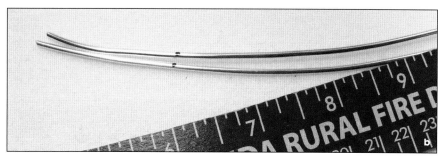

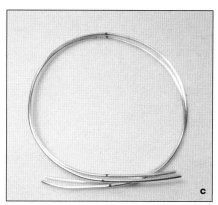

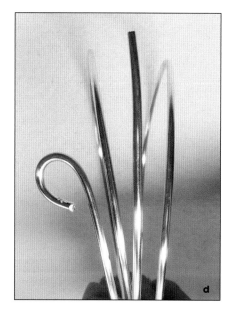

Instructions

1. Measure your upper arm where you want to wear the armlet. This is measurement #1. Add 3" to measurement #1 to determine the final length of wire you need. This will be measurement #2. Cut two pieces of 12-gauge wire the length of measurement #2.

2. Make a small mark at the center of each wire **(a)**. From the center point, make a small mark half the distance of measurement #1 on each wire. This mark should be approximately 1¾" from each end **(b)**.

3. Hold both lengths of wire side by side, lining up the marks made in the previous step. Using your fingers, and taking your time, gently bend the wires into a circular shape. Each end's marks should almost meet with the ends overlapping **(c)**.

4. Position chainnose pliers near the end of one of the wires and bend the end of the wire out to either side **(d)**. Using the pliers (or your fingers), continue to bend the wire in the design of your choice, stopping near the mark made in step 2 **(e)**.

5. Work as in step 4 for the each of the remaining ends **(f)**.

6. Cut a 3–4" length of 20-gauge wire. Using flatnose pliers, make a bend in the wire approximately 8mm from one end **(g)**. This makes a small hook **(h)**.

7. Holding the wires in the armlet together, place the hook over both wires at the mark in the center. It may help to hold the hook with flatnose pliers **(i)**.

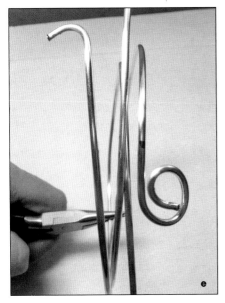

e

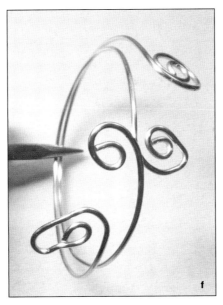

f

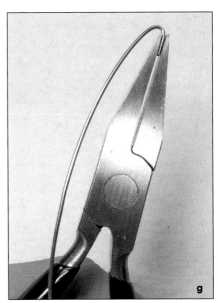

g

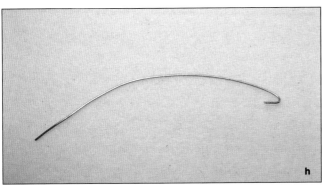

h

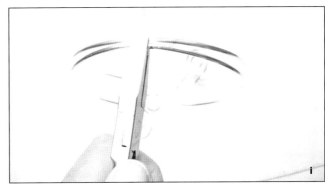

i

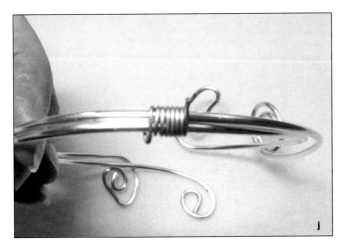

j

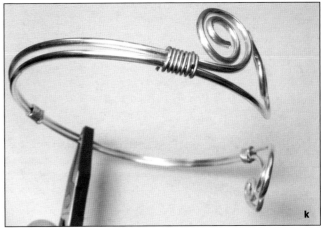

k

8. Wrap the 20-gauge wire tightly around both wires in the armlet. Continue to wrap the wire, keeping your wraps close together for six or seven wraps, ending with the wire to the outside of the armlet. Trim the wire and press the end in to the armlet **(j)**.

TIP Do not press the wire to the underside of the armlet, as it will scratch when worn.

9. Repeat steps 6–8 near the mark at each end of the armlet **(k)**.

10. Open the jump ring on the charm and attach to the decorative coils on one end of the armlet **(Basics, p. 109)**.

TIP Use rubbing alcohol or a baby wipe to remove the marker from the wire if necessary.

Vassal's brooch

A good vassal serves his lord faithfully, and a generous master richly rewards his subject's fealty. He may even bestow the honor of carrying the kingdom's banner to this trusted liege —a high honor, indeed.

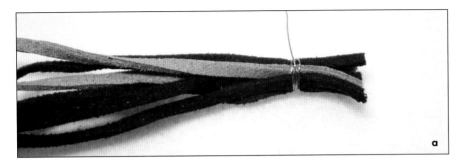

a

b

MATERIALS & TOOLS

- Wolf charm *(or other embellishment of your choosing)*
- 9' 3mm suede cord, color A
- 3' 3mm suede cord, color B
- 16" 28-gauge wire
- Fireline 6 lb. test
- 2" felt circle
- Pin back finding

- Beading needle #10
- E6000 glue
- Kumihimo disk
- Scissors
- Sharpie marker
- Small clamps, bulldog clips, or clothes pins
- White craft glue

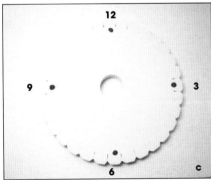

c

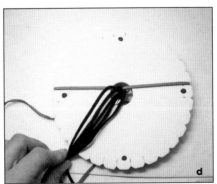

d

Instructions

Preparing the cords

1. Cut six 18" lengths of color A cord. Cut two 18" lengths of color B cord.

2. Cut an 8" length of 28-gauge wire. Bundle the cords together and wrap the wire tightly around all eight cords, approximately ½" from one end **(a)**.

3. Place the clamp around the ends of the cord near the wrap **(b)**.

Preparing the braids

1. Turn the kumihimo disk to the back and make four dots with a marker on the disk.

These will be your guides. Select one dot to be the top dot. If necessary, make your own mark so you know this is the top. For the purposes of these instructions, we will call the top dot "12 o'clock." Moving clockwise, we will call the next dot "3 o'clock," the next dot "6 o'clock," and the final dot "9 o'clock" **(c)**.

2. Insert the clamp through the center of the Kumihimo disk. Position one of the color B cords in the slot above the 9 o'clock dot and position the other color B cord in the slot above the 3 o'clock dot **(d)**.

e

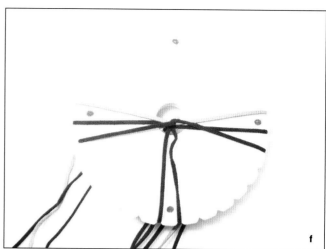

f

g

h

3. Position the color A cords in the remaining slots as shown **(e)**.

Braid

The directions given here are based on a clockwise direction so I have underlined the key position indicator of <u>before</u> and <u>after</u> as it relates to the dot.

1. Pick up the cord immediately <u>after</u> the 12 o'clock dot and move it down to the first available slot <u>before</u> the 9 o'clock dot. Pick up the cord immediately <u>before</u> the 12 o'clock dot and move it down to the first available slot <u>after</u> the 3 o'clock dot **(f)**.

2. Pick up the cord immediately <u>before</u> the 6 o'clock dot and move it up to the first available slot <u>after</u> the 9 o'clock slot **(g)**.

3. Pick up the cord immediately <u>after</u> the 6 o'clock dot and move it up to the first available slot <u>before</u> the 3 o'clock dot **(h)**. (I call these "cat whiskers.")

TIP If for any reason you have to set your work down, this is a good stopping point, as you can easily locate the cord for the next move.

4. Pick up the cord immediately <u>before</u> the 9 o'clock slot and move it up to the first available slot <u>before</u> the 12 o'clock dot **(i)**.

5. Pick up the cord immediately <u>after</u> the 3 o'clock slot and move it up to the first available slot <u>after</u> the 12 o'clock dot **(j)**.

6. Pick up the cord immediately <u>after</u> the 9 o'clock slot and move it down to the first available slot <u>after</u> the 6 o'clock dot **(k)**.

7. Pick up the cord immediately <u>before</u> the 3 o'clock slot and move it down to the first available slot <u>before</u> the 6 o'clock dot **(l)** .

8. Reposition the cords at the 3 o'clock and 6 o'clock positions to the slots immediately <u>before</u> and <u>after</u> the respective dots .This completes one cycle of the braid. Notice that you have cords in the same slots you started with **(m)**.

9. Repeat Steps 1–9 until the braid measures approximately 7" long.

10. Cut an 8" length of 28-gauge wire.

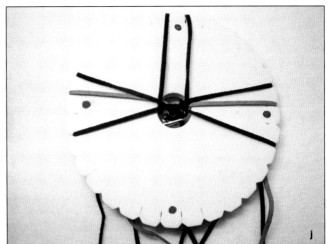

11. Carefully remove the cords from the disk and wrap the wire tightly around the cords at the end of the braid **(n)**.

12. Trim the cord ends to 2½–3″.

Brooch assembly

1. Using one of the scrap cords you just cut off, wrap it around the braid a few times to hide the wire wraps and tie a knot on the back of the braid **(n)**. Secure it with a dot of E6000.

2. Trim the cords at the beginning end close to the wire wraps. Apply E6000 to approximately 1″ of the front of the braid at this end. Make sure to apply the glue to the cut ends and the wire wrap **(o)**.

3. Form the braid into a 2″ circle with the loose ends overlapping the beginning end **(p)**. Clamp the overlapping sections of the braid and set aside to dry for at least 15 minutes. Once dry, remove the clamp.

4. Apply white glue along the outer edges of the 2″ felt circle **(q)**. Position the braid on the felt circle and press the edges together **(r)**. Secure with a clamp and allow it to dry.

TIP Even though the felt has been glued to the braid, I always whip stitch it to the braid for extra security.

5. Position the pin back finding on the back of the felt. Tie an overhand knot **(Basics p. 110)** at one end of 8″ of thread and make a small stitch in the felt near the pin back finding to secure it. Using small stitches, sew the pin back finding to the felt through the small holes in the pin back finding **(s)**.

6. Sew through to the front of the pin and sew the charm of your choice onto the felt inside the braided frame **(t)**. Sew through to the back and end the thread with white glue along the outer edges of the 2″ felt circle.

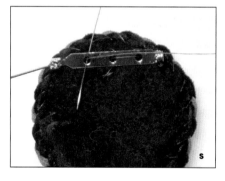

designer NOTE

You can magically turn this brooch into a pendant by leaving off the felt backing and pin finding. Attach a large charm to the front of the braided circle with jump rings and slide it onto a ready-made necklace chain.

Necklaces

Prisoner's Chain necklace

Trapped in the deepest dungeon, a captured rival awaits his fate. He dreams of fleeing to the arms of his beloved in a daring escape. But for now, the executioner's block awaits.

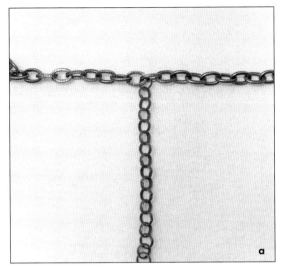

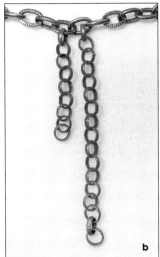

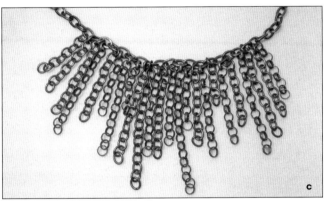

MATERIALS & TOOLS

- 16" 11x7mm textured-link, medium-thick chain, bronze

- 3" extender chain and dangle, bronze

- 30" 7mm rolo chain, medium-thick, bronze

- 27" 9x7mm medium thick chain, bronze

- **2** 6mm jump rings, bronze

- Lobster claw clasp, bronze

- **2** pairs chainnose pliers

- Wire cutters

Instructions

Preparation

1. Cut the 7mm rolo chain into the following lengths:

> **1** length, 17 links long
> **3** lengths, 14 links long
> **2** lengths, 12 links long
> **2** lengths, 11 links long
> **4** lengths, 9 links long

2. Cut the 9x7mm link chain into the following lengths:

> **1** length, 15 links long
> **1** length, 13 links long
> **1** length, 12 links long
> **2** lengths, 11 links long
> **3** lengths, 10 links long
> **2** lengths, 9 links long
> **1** length, 8 links long
> **1** length, 5 links long

Assembly

1. Locate the center link of the 16″ 11x7mm base chain. Open an end link of the 17-link length of rolo chain and attach to the center link in the base chain. Close the link **(Basics, p. 109) (a)**.

2. Open an end link of a 9-link chain and attach it to an adjacent link in the base chain **(b)**. Repeat to add a 9- and 12-link piece of chain on the other side of the center link.

3. Continue adding lengths of rolo chain, alternating long and short from the center out towards the ends. Use only the links of the center 6" of the base chain. Occasionally skip a link or two between dangles.

4. Continue filling in the center 6" of base chain by attaching various lengths of the 9x7mm link chain **(c)**. (Don't be afraid to attach the 9x7mm chain to the same base chain links where you have already attached a rolo chain.)

5. Open a 6mm jump ring and attach the end link of the base chain and the lobster claw clasp **(d)**. Close the loop.

6. Open a 6mm jump ring and attach the end link of the extender chain if needed. Close the loop.

The Chieftain choker

Strength, cunning, and bravery: these are the hallmarks of a worthy clan chief. Lead your men in battle, and claim glory for your tribe.

Instructions

Stone pendant

1. Cut two 8" lengths of 24-gauge Artistic wire.

2. Position a pair of roundnose pliers in the center of one wire, and bend both ends around the pliers **(a)**. Cross the wires together to make a loop.

3. With one end of the wire, make six or seven wraps around the other wire just below the loop. These wraps should cover approximately 6mm of the wire. You now have one long wire (the lead wire) and one short wire (the tail wire).

4. Remove the pliers and position the loop along the upper edge of the stone spear. If the spear has a hole, string the long end of the wire through the hole **(b)**. Wrap each end of the wire tightly around the stone spear two or three times near the end of the spear **(c)**.

designer NOTE

For a more feminine-looking choker, use smaller beads and a crystal spear.

MATERIALS & TOOLS

- **40** 10mm shell disks
- **36** 3x6mm lentil stone beads
- **7** 8x25mm dark stained wood barrel beads
- **6** 8x10mm stained wood beehive beads
- **4** 5x10mm top-drilled stone spear
- 26" Accu-Flex 49 strand beading wire (.014 diameter)
- 16" 24-gauge Artistic wire, silver
- **2** crimp beads
- **2** crimp covers *(optional)*
- 6mm jump ring
- Lobster claw clasp

- Flatnose pliers
- Roundnose pliers
- Wire cutters

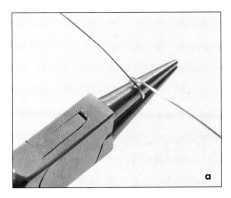

a

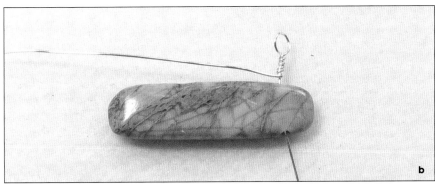

b

c

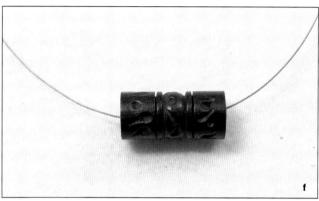

5. Make several wraps around the wraps made in step **3.** Trim the wire and press the ends flat against your work with flatnose pliers, making sure the wrapped loop is perpendicular to the spear and in the correct position for stringing **(d)**.

6. Work as in steps 1–5 using the other 8" wire and the available end of the spear **(e)**.

Necklace assembly

1. Center an 8mm wood barrel bead on the beading wire **(f)**.

2. On each end, string a 3x6mm lentil stone bead and a loop of the stone pendant **(g)**.

3. On one end, string a barrel bead, a 10mm shell disk, a 3x6mm bead, a 10mm disk, a beehive bead, three 10mm disks, a 3x6mm bead, three 10mm disks, a barrel bead, a 10mm disk, a 3x6mm bead, a 10mm disk, a beehive bead, a 10mm disk, a 3x6mm bead, a 10mm disk, a barrel bead, a 10mm disk, a 3x6mm bead, a 10mm disk, a beehive bead, three 10mm disks, a 3x6mm bead, three 10mm disks, and 11 3x6mm beads **(h)**.

4. Repeat step 3 on the other end of the beading wire.

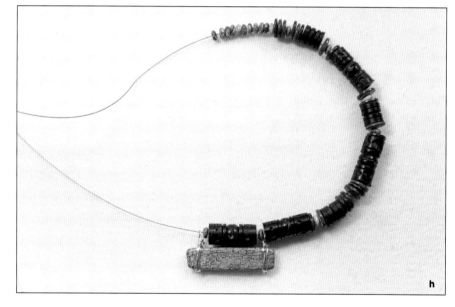

5. On one end of the beading wire, string a crimp bead and a lobster claw clasp. Go back through the crimp bead and snug up the wire to form a small loop.

6. Make a flat or folded crimp, and trim the wire **(Basics, p. 109)**. Add a crimp cover if desired **(Basics, p. 109)**.

7. On the available end of the beading wire, string a crimp bead and a 6mm jump ring. Go back through the crimp bead and snug up the wire to form a small loop.

8. Work as in step 6 to complete this side.

Ancient Dragonfly necklace

Beside a babbling brook, a comely maiden pines for her betrothed. As if in answer to her plea, a small winged creature alights upon her shoulder.

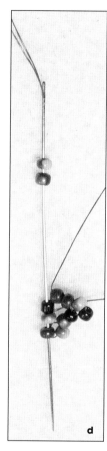

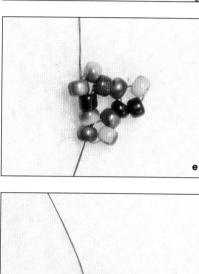

Instructions

1. Pour the seed bead mix onto your beading surface. On a comfortable length of Fireline, pick up six 11º seed beads from the mix. Tie the beads into a ring with a square knot **(Basics, p. 110)**, leaving an 8" tail **(a)**. Sew through the first bead again **(b)**.

2. Pick up two 11ºs, and sew through the next two 11ºs in the original ring **(c)**. Repeat this step two more times, but in the last repeat, step up through the first 11º picked up in this step **(d)**. You now have three 2-bead columns **(e)**.

3. Pick up two 11ºs, sew down through the next 11º in this column, and up through the first 11º in the next column **(f)**. Repeat twice, but in the last repeat, step up through the first 11º added in this step as well **(g)**. **Photo h** shows your work before you snug up the beads; you can clearly see the three columns. Once you snug up your beads **(i)**, the beads begin to form a tube.

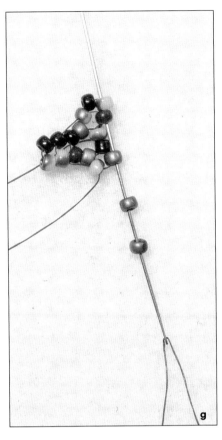

4. Work as in step 3 until the rope measures 16" long, ending and adding Fireline **(Basics, p. 110)** as needed.

5. Sew through all six beads in the last round twice, pick up a cone, an 8º seed bead, and five 11º copper seed beads **(j)**. Continue through the 8º and five copper 11ºs to form a ring **(k)**. Retrace the threadpath several times and exit the 8º. Sew back down through the cone and the rope. End the thread.

6. Thread a needle on the tail, and work as in steps 6 and 7 on this end of the necklace.

7. Open an 8mm jump ring **(Basics, p. 109)**. Attach a beaded loop on one end of the necklace. Close the jump ring **(l)**.

8. Open an 8mm jump ring and attach the S-hook and the beaded loop on the available end of the necklace. Close the jump ring.

9. Open the 10mm jump ring and attach the dragonfly charm and the necklace **(m)**. Close the jump ring.

Tangled Roots choker

Like the roots of ancient trees, gnarled and twisted together, an ancient pattern emerges. Deep wine and mysterious, the entwined branches combine in an unending tangle.

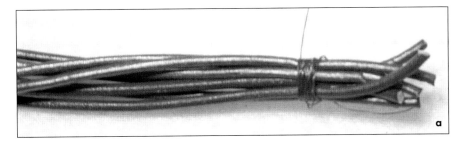

a

Instructions

Preparing the disk

1. Cut an 8" length of Fireline. Group all eight cords into a bundle. Make sure the ends are even, and wrap the Fireline around the cords several times approximately ½" from the end. Secure with an overhand knot **(Basics, p. 110) (a)**.

2. Hold the ends of the cords together with the clamp. Insert the clamp through the center of the Kumihimo disk.

3. Make four large dots on the disk; these will be your guides. Select one dot to be the top dot. (If helpful, make a mark so you know this is the top.)

For the purposes of these instructions, we will call the top dot "12 o'clock." Moving clockwise, we will call the next dot "3 o'clock," the next dot "6 o'clock," and the final dot "9 o'clock."

4. Position one of the color B cords in the slot above the 9 o'clock dot; position the other color B cord in the slot above the 3 o'clock dot.

5. Position the color A cords in the slots as shown in **(b)**.

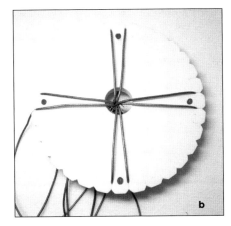

b

Braid

The directions given here are based on a clockwise direction; so I have underlined the key position indicators of before and after as it relates to the dot.

1. Pick up the cord immediately <u>before</u> the 12 o'clock dot and move it down to the first available slot <u>after</u> the 3 o'clock dot **(c)**.

2. Pick up the cord immediately <u>after</u> the 12 o'clock dot and move it down to the first available slot <u>before</u> the 9 o'clock dot **(d)**.

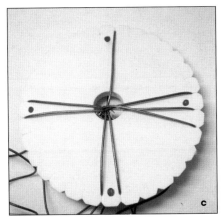

c

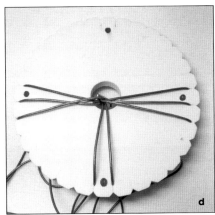

d

MATERIALS & TOOLS

- 34mm dragon charm
- **6** 3' lengths 3mm leather cord, color A
- **2** 3' lengths 3mm leather cord, color B
- 12" 20-gauge twisted wire, copper
- **2** 10x28mm hammered copper end cones
- **4** 6mm jump rings, copper
- 12mm textured ring, copper
- 8mm split ring, copper
- 30mm lobster claw clasp, copper
- Fireline 6-lb. test

- **2** pairs chainnose pliers
- Clamps, bulldog clips, or clothes pins
- E6000
- Kumihimo disk
- Roundnose pliers
- Scissors
- Sharpie marker
- Wire cutters

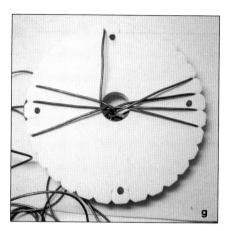

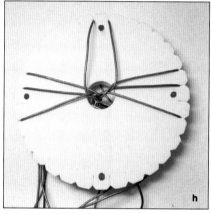

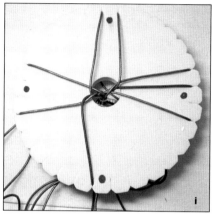

3. Pick up the cord immediately <u>before</u> the 6 o'clock dot and move it up to the first available slot <u>after</u> the 9 o'clock slot **(e)**.

4. Pick up the cord immediately <u>after</u> the 6 o'clock dot and move it up to the first available slot <u>before</u> the 3 o'clock dot **(f)**. You now have "cat whiskers." It's good to stop for a moment and consider your position on the disk. If you need a stopping point during the braiding portion of this project, this is the place to stop. You can easily pick up from the "cat whiskers."

5. Pick up the cord immediately <u>before</u> the 9 o'clock slot and move it up to the first available slot <u>before</u> the 12 o'clock dot **(g)**.

6. Pick up the cord immediately <u>after</u> the 3 o'clock slot and move it up to the first available slot <u>after</u> the 12 o'clock dot **(h)**.

7. Pick up the cord immediately <u>after</u> the 9 o'clock slot and move it down to the first available slot <u>after</u> the 6 o'clock dot **(i)**.

8. Pick up the cord immediately <u>before</u> the 3 o'clock slot and move it down to the first available slot <u>before</u> the 6 o'clock dot **(j)**.

9. Reposition the cords at the 3 o'clock and 9 o'clock positions to the slots immediately <u>before</u> and <u>after</u> the respective dots **(k)**. This completes one cycle of the braid. Notice that you have cords in the same slots you started with.

10. Repeat steps 1–9 until the braid measures approximately 12".

TIP Stretch the braid so the weave falls into place and the tension evens out, making sure not to pull the cords out of the slots.

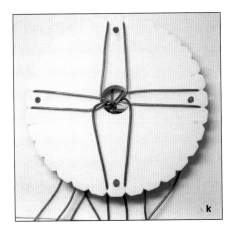

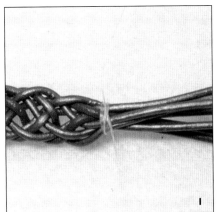

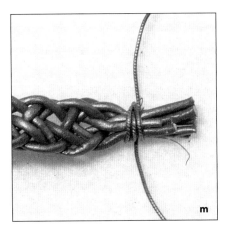

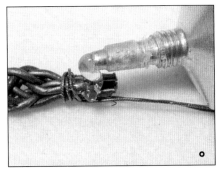

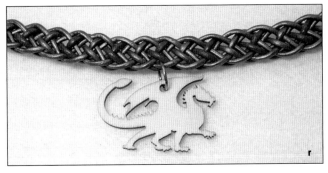

11. Cut an 8" length of Fireline. Carefully remove the cords from the disk, wrap the thread tightly around the cords several times near the end of the braid, and secure with an overhand knot **(l)**.

12. Trim the cord ends to about ½".

Assembly

1. Cut the twisted copper wire into two equal lengths.

2. Center one wire over the cords on top of the thread, and wrap both ends tightly around the cord two or three times **(m)**.

3. Bring both ends of the wire together past the end of the braid **(n)**.

4. Apply a layer of E6000 to the wire, thread, and cord ends **(o)**.

5. Slide an end cone over both ends of wire, and push it down over the end of the braid. Make sure the cone covers the wire **(p)**. Allow the glue to dry.

6. Using roundnose pliers, grasp both wires exiting the end cone. Make a wrapped loop **(Basics, p. 108)**. Trim the wires **(q)**.

7. Open a 6mm jump ring **(Basics, p. 109)** and attach the wrapped loop and a 12mm textured ring. Close the ring. Repeat with another 6mm jump ring.

8. Repeat steps 1–7 for the other end of the necklace, but in step 7, attach the jump rings to the wrapped loop and a lobster claw clasp.

9. Locate the center of the braid. Open a split ring **(Basics, p. 109)** and attach it to the bottom cord of the braid. Slide the jump ring of the dragon charm through the split ring. Close the ring **(r)**.

Stonehenge necklace

Misty shadows fall across the land, but you do not fear. In this place, the souls of your ancestors surround you and fill you with strength.

Instructions

1. Cut the 8–10" chain into two equal pieces.

2. Select the shortest crystal spike. Center the spike on the piece of 22-gauge silver wire. Using chainnose pliers, make a 90-degree bend on each side of the spike. With your fingers, bring the ends of the wire up and cross above the spike. Using roundnose pliers, make the first half of a wrapped loop **(Basics, p. 108)**. Attach an end link of the extender chain to the loop and complete the wrap. Wrap the remaining end of the wire around the base of the loop to make a messy wrap around the dangle **(a)**. Tuck in the ends of the wire.

3. Sort the crystal spikes from longest to shortest **(b)**. String the longest spike onto the center of the beading wire. On each end, string a 4mm bicone crystal **(c)**.

a

b

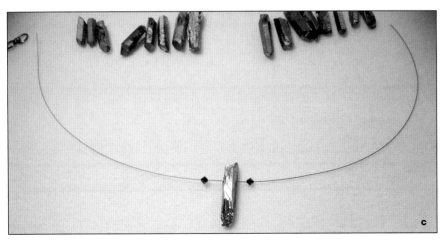

c

MATERIALS & TOOLS

- **18** top-drilled 15–16mm metallic-coated crystal stick spikes
- **18** 4mm bicone crystals, black
- **2** crimp beads, silver
- 12" stainless steel beading wire
- 8–10" length of chain, silver (8mm links)
- 4" 22-gauge wire, silver
- 1½" extender chain, silver
- **2** crimp bead covers, silver *(optional)*
- **2** 4mm jump rings, silver
- Lobster claw clasp, silver

- Crimping pliers
- Chainnose pliers
- Roundnose pliers
- Wire cutters

4. On each end, string the next longest spike and a 4mm. Continue in this manner, using progressively shorter crystal spikes, until you have strung 17 crystal spikes. End with a 4mm on each end.

5. On one end, string a crimp bead and the end link of a 4–5" length of chain. Pass the wire back through the crimp and the nearest 4mm, leaving a small loop **(d)**. Crimp the crimp bead. Attach a crimp cover if desired **(e)** and trim the beading wire close to the 4mm bead **(Basics, p. 109)**.

6. Work as in step 2 for the remaining end, but snug up the beads before crimping.

7. With the pliers, open a 4mm jump ring and attach the lobster claw clasp to the available end of the necklace **(Basics, p. 109)**. Close the ring **(f)**.

8. Open the remaining jump ring and attach the available end of the necklace to the end link in the extender chain.

TIP I generally use an extender chain because I like to be able to shorten or lengthen my necklace depending on my neckline. It's entirely optional.

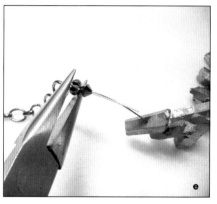

designer NOTES

Quartz crystal stick spikes are available in a variety of metallic finishes with which to experiment. Select a color that compliments your aura.

For a variation, use two 12" or longer lengths of small link chain in place of the 8mm link chain. Substitute 11º seed beads in place of the 4mm beads, and use nine dyed stone spikes instead of 17 crystal spikes for a longer necklace.

Mystic Crystal necklace

The key to the drawbridge hides within the crystals framing your neck. Unlock the bridge, cross the moat, and leave the tower behind — forever!

- **9** top-drilled mystic crystal sticks
- **9** 57mm metal filigree components
- 6' 28-gauge Parawire, gun metal
- Chinese cord neckwire with clasp

- Chainnose pliers
- Metal hole punch
- Pencil
- Wire cutters

a

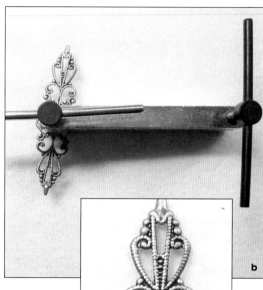

b

c

Instructions

1. Using a metal hole punch, punch a small hole in the center of a metal filigree component **(photos a, b, and c)**.

2. With the right side of the component facing you, position a pair of chainnose pliers just above the hole you created in step 1 **(d)**. Using your fingers, gently bend the top ⅓ of the component toward you at a 90-degree angle **(e)**.

3. Place a pencil above the bent portion, and using your fingers, wrap the bent portion of the component back around the pencil to form a bail **(f)**. Remove the pencil.

TIP If your cord is thinner than the cord I used, adjust the bail on each filigree component so the loop is smaller.

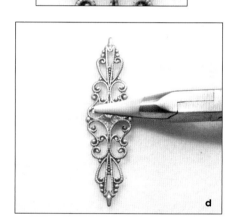

d

designer NOTE

I believe in using what I have on hand, and I enjoy experimentation. The basic technique here is to make a hole in the filigree component and wire wrap something to the front of the component. If you don't have crystal sticks, play around with stick pearls, crystal briolettes, long dagger beads, or foreign coins in place of crystal sticks. Have fun with it!

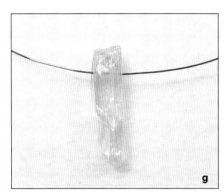

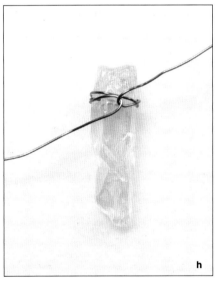

4. Cut an 8" length of 28-gauge Parawire and center a crystal stick on the wire **(g)**.
5. Wrap each end of the wire around the crystal several times, then cross the wires at the back of the crystal **(h)**.
6. Thread the wire through the center hole in the filigree component and snug the crystal to the component **(i)**.
7. Wrap each end of the wire snugly through the filigree and around the crystal several more times. Trim the ends of the wire, tuck them around the edge of the crystal, and secure using chainnose pliers, if necessary **(j)**.

8. Repeat steps 1–7 eight times for a total of nine crystal-and-filigree components.
9. String the components on a Chinese cord neckwire.

TIP The crystal sticks may vary quite a bit in length and width, so before you string the crystal filigree components onto the necklace, arrange them by size with the largest in the center and the smallest on the ends. It's easier if you string the largest first and work out from the center.

Magic Ring lariat

The spirit of Merlin embraces your being. Magic rings, stars, and mystic tubes declare your birthright.

a

Instructions

Lariat ends

1. On a headpin, string an 8° seed bead, a stamped tube, and an 8° bead. Make the first half of a wrapped loop **(Basics, p. 108)**. Attach an end link of the chain to the loop, and complete the wraps **(a)**.

2. String the other end of the chain through the center of the alchemy rock **(b)**. Open a jump ring **(Basics, p. 109)**. Attach the end link of the chain and the 9th link from the same end **(c)**. Close the jump ring.

MATERIALS & TOOLS

- **2** 8° seed beads, blue
- 2g 11° seed beads, color A
- 1g 11° seed beads, color B
- 36mm stamped tube, silver
- 34mm alchemy rock, silver (www.greengirl-studios.com)
- 30" chain with 5mm links, silver
- 6mm jump ring, silver
- 2" headpin, silver
- Fireline 6-lb. test

- Beading needle #10
- Chainnose pliers
- Roundnose pliers
- Scissors

b

c

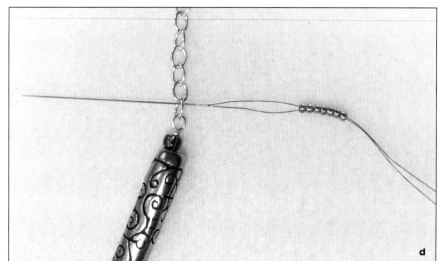

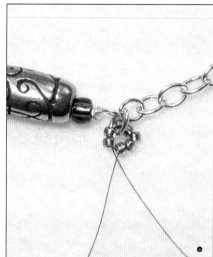

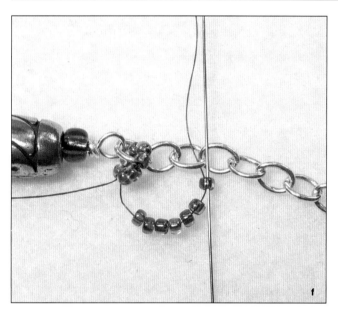

Chain embellishment

1. On a comfortable length of Fireline, pick up seven color B 11º seed beads and the first link of the chain on the end with the stamped tube **(d)**. Tie the ends together with a square knot **(Basics, p. 110)** to form a ring, leaving a 6" tail. Sew through all the beads several times to secure **(e)**.

2. Pick up three color A 11º seed beads, a B, three As, then skip a link in the chain. Sew through the following link in the chain and back through the last A added **(f)**.

3. Pick up two As, a B, three As, then skip a link in the chain. Sew through the following link in the chain, and back through the last A again **(g)**. Repeat this step to embellish the entire chain, but in the last repeat, pick up seven Bs and the next link in the chain by the alchemy rock. Sew through all seven Bs several times, and tie two half-hitch knots to secure. End the threads **(Basics, p. 110)**.

Claw and Crystal Torque necklace

M'Lady exhibits power with the clan's abalone claw at her throat. Serfs and commoners make way as she passes in triumph.

MATERIALS & TOOLS

- **62** 11º seed beads, gold
- **31** 6mm fire-polished beads
- 16x30mm abalone charm
- 72" 24-gauge Artistic wire, gold
- 54" 12-gauge braided wire, gold
- 3" chain with 5mm oval links, gold
- 5mm jump ring, gold

- Chainnose pliers
- Roundnose pliers
- Wire cutters

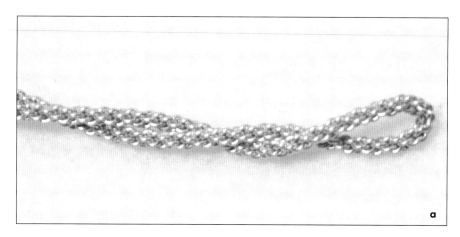

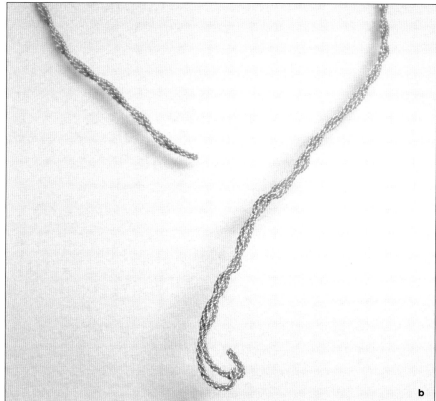

Instructions

1. Fold the braided wire in half. The fold should create a small loop. Twist the wire around itself, using two pairs of pliers if necessary, to get a tight twist without kinking **(a)**.

2. Form the braided wire into a circle large enough to fit around your neck. The folded end should begin at the middle of your neck, and the tail end should overlap the folded end by 2–2½" **(b)**. Trim the tail end of the wire as needed.

3. Using roundnose pliers and/or your fingers, grasp the tail of the braided wires and form a coil. Continue to coil the braid back on itself **(c)**.

4. Wrap one end of the 24-gauge wire (the wrapping wire) around the braided wire several times at the base of the loop created in step 1. Make sure the wraps cover the tail of the 24-gauge wire **(d)**.

5. Bring the wrapping wire to the outside of the braided wire and pick up an 11° seed bead, a 6mm fire-polished bead, and an 11°. Continue the wrap **(e)**. Make two more wraps next to the last wrap.

6. Work as in steps 4 and 5 for the length of the twisted braid, stopping at the point where the fold meets the tail. Make several wraps; trim the wire; press the ends to your work with the pliers.

7. Open a 5mm jump ring and attach the loop of the fold and one end of the chain. Close the ring **(Basics, p. 109)**.

8. Attach the other end of the chain to the abalone claw **(f)**.

9. Manipulate the wire as necessary so it lays the way you desire on your neck.

c

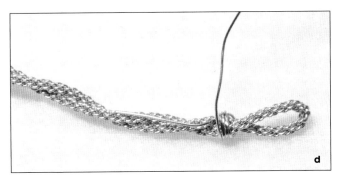

d

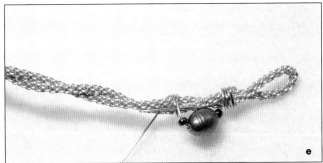

e

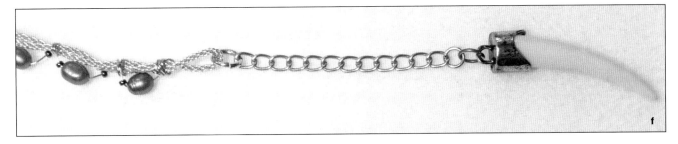

f

designer NOTE

This necklace is designed for the abalone claw to rest in the middle of your neck. Don't be afraid to trim and bend the coil so it lays flat.

Fortune Teller's necklace

Dreams, fascinations, and infatuations create her mysterious personality. Your brave knight's failure to return from the battlefield urges you to seek her power.

a

b

d

c

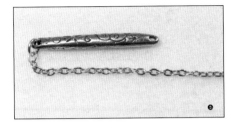

e

f

g

h

MATERIALS & TOOLS

- **44–50** jump rings, silver, assorted sizes: 8mm, 6,mm, 4mm
- **12–15** rings of various sizes
- **10–15** charms and/or small pendants
- **8–10** 4-25mm beads
- **8–10** links, silver
- 3' chain, silver
- 24-gauge wire, spool, silver
- 22-gauge wire, spool, silver
- Lobster claw clasp, silver (optional, depending on the length of your necklace)
- Variety of seed beads, spacer beads, and bead caps

- Beading awl
- **2** pairs chainnose pliers
- Roundnose pliers
- Wire cutters

Instructions

Here is your chance to explore and create a truly one-of-a-kind necklace. Select a handful of items that speak to you, and using the techniques described, wrap them with wire, embellish them with chain, or suspend them in the center of a ring. Choose bits and baubles that represent your unique style and link them together with wrapped loops and jump rings.

Bead Links

1. Cut a 2½–3" length of 22-gauge wire. On one end, make a wrapped loop with roundnose pliers **(Basics, p. 108)** and trim the wire.

2. Add a bead cap from top to bottom, a bead of your choice, and a bead cap from bottom to top.

3. Make a wrapped loop with roundnose pliers. Trim the wire with wire cutters **(a)**.

4. To connect subsequent bead links without jump rings, make a second bead link as in steps 1 and 2. In step 3, make the first half of a wrapped loop, attach the loop of another bead link or a ring, and complete the wraps **(b)**.

5. For bead links, work as in steps 1 and 2 above, but in step 2, add seed beads and/or spacer beads before and after the focal bead **(c)**. Then work as in step 3 or 4 depending on your design.

Chain embellishment with dangle

1. Cut a length of chain approximately 1" longer than the bead or link you wish to embellish **(d)**.

2. Open a jump ring and attach the link and an end link in the chain. Close the ring **(e)**.

3. Position the chain along the link so that it hangs away from the link slightly **(f)**. Open a jump ring and attach the other end of the link and the nearest link in the chain. Close the ring **(g)**.

4. Open a 4 mm jump ring and attach a charm to the available end of the chain **(h)**.

Caged bead

1. Cut a 5–6" length of 22-gauge wire. On one end, make a wrapped loop.

2. Add an 8–10mm bead or pearl and make a wrapped loop. Do not trim the wire **(i)**.

3. Using your fingers, wrap the tail around the bead twice in a spiral **(j)**. Wrap the wire a few times around the first wrapped loop, and trim the wire if necessary **(k)**.

Floating bead

1. Select a bead that is 4–5mm smaller than the inside diameter of a ring **(l)**.

2. Cut a 3" length of 22-gauge wire. On one end of the wire, make the first half of a wrapped loop, attach the ring, and complete the wraps.

3. Add the bead and make a single wrap around the ring opposite the wrapped loop **(m)**. This serves as the first half of a wrapped loop.

4. Complete the wraps and trim the wire.

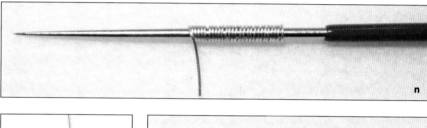

Coiled wire component

1. Cut a 24" length of 24-gauge wire. Beginning at one end and using your fingers, carefully wrap the wire tightly around a beading awl **(n)**, making sure the wraps are close together. Continue to coil the wire around the awl until you reach the end of the wire. Remove the coiled wire from the awl.

2. Cut a 2" length of wire. On one end, make a wrapped loop. Add a 6º seed bead and the coiled wire **(o)**. Using your fingers, form the coiled wire into a teardrop shape and add a large ring or link.

3. Make a few wraps with the available end of the wire at the base of the seed bead **(p)**.

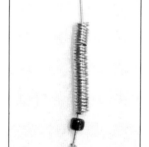

designer NOTE

Make as many or as few of these components as you desire; sprinkle them among lengths of chain, rings, and links as your creative spirit dictates. I recommend trying the necklace on as you work to determine which way the charms will fall. Don't hesitate to use different beads, charms, chains, and rings to make it clear this piece is all about you!

Bracelets

Forever Entwined cuff

Placing the bracelet upon her wrist, she is wrapped in the finery of her true love's favor. Though he sails the seas, their hearts are braided in eternal devotion.

Instructions

Knotted braid

1. Pair the cords together; fold them in half and tie an overhand knot **(Basics, p. 110)**, leaving a small loop **(a)**.

2. Separate the cords into pairs consisting of one black cord and one copper cord each. (For the purposes of these instructions, we will label them "left cords" and "right cords," and each set will be worked together as if they were one cord.)

3. With the left cords, make a loop by bringing the cord in toward the center, up and out to the left of your work surface **(b)**.

4. Lay the right cords over the center of the loop created in the previous step **(c)**, and bring the right cords out to the left and up under the tail of the left cords **(d)**.

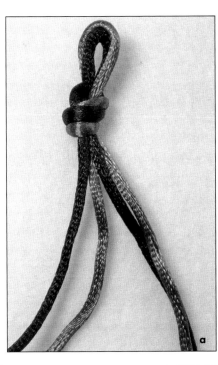

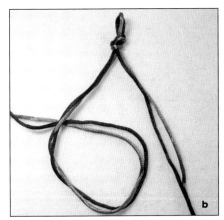

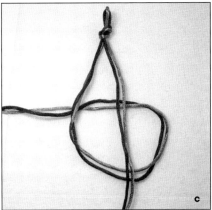

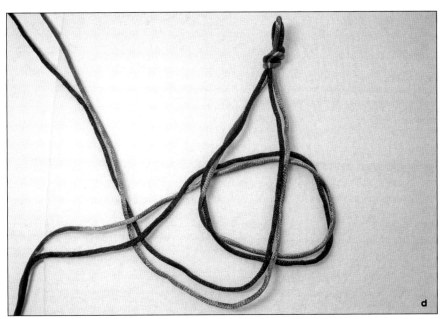

MATERIALS & TOOLS

- 6' satin cord, black
- 6' satin cord, copper
- 3' 26-gauge wire
- Premade metal filigree cuff

- Flatnose pliers *(optional)*
- Wire cutters

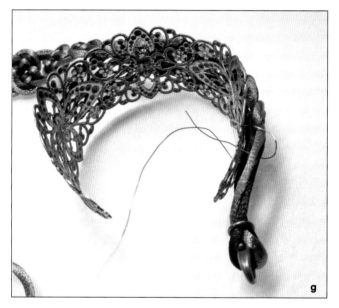

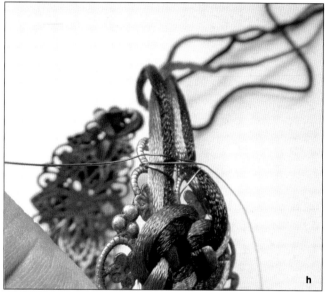

5. Refer to **photo e,** and work from left to right across your work surface. With the cords used in step 4, cross over the nearest left cords, under the loop of the left cords created in step 3, over the right cords as they lay through the center of the loop, and under the loop of the left cords.

6. Snug up the cords to within ¾" of the overhand knot, carefully adjusting them as desired **(f)**. I chose to keep the black cords to the inside of my knot.

7. Repeat steps 3–6 seven times, snugging up each knot to within ½" of the previous knot.

8. Tie an overhand knot with the tails.

Assembly

1. Center the knotted cord on the filigree cuff. Cut a comfortable length of 26-gauge wire. Working from the center out toward each end, thread the wire up through the cuff, over the cord, and back down through the cuff **(g)**. Repeat with each end of the cord to secure the braid to the cuff.

2. Flatten the wire to the cuff using flat-nose pliers, if necessary. Trim the wire.

3. Cut a 4" length of wire. Wrap the wire several times around the ends of the cord at one end of the cuff , and secure the wire to the cuff **(h)**. Repeat on the opposite end of the braid.

designer NOTE
Experiment with soutache braid or thin leather cording in place of the satin cord.

Mystic Warrior cuff

Through the smoke of the battlefield, an unlikely hero arises. A crash of thunder and the glint of a sword invokes the spirit of fallen dragons of old.

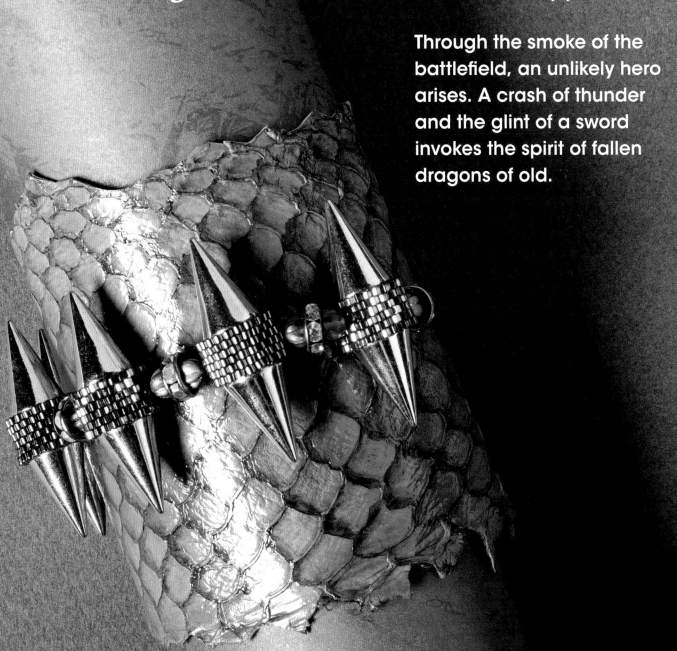

MATERIALS & TOOLS

- **6g** 11º cylinder beads, Iris light bronze
- **2** 11º round seed beads, Iris metallic bronze
- **12** 4mm melon beads, metallic
- **10** 10x20mm spike beads, silver
- **6** 8mm rhinestone spacers, antique brass
- Fireline 6-lb. test
- 8–10" fish leather

- Beading needle #10
- Bench block
- Chasing hammer
- Leather punch
- Scissors
- Snap set and setting tool
- Super New Glue

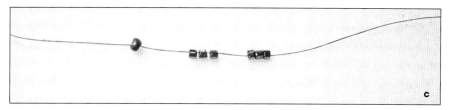

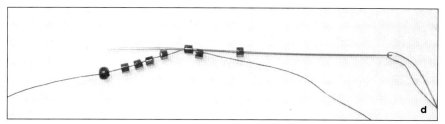

Instructions

Spike Units

1. On the flat end of a spike bead, apply a dab or two of Super New Glue **(a)**. Line up the holes of a second spike bead with the holes in the spike bead where you applied glue, and press the flat ends of each spike together to form a double-pointed spike unit **(b)**. Hold in place for 30 seconds and set side.
2. Work as in step 1 for a total of five spike units.

Beaded bands

Work in flat even-count peyote stitch to create a band that is six beads wide and 46 rows long.
1. Thread a needle and attach a stop bead on a comfortable length of Fireline **(Basics, p 110)**, and pick up six 11º cylinder beads **(c)**. Leave a 6" tail. These beads will shift to form the first two rows as the third row is added.
2. Pick up an 11º cylinder, skip the last 11º cylinder, and sew through the next 11º cylinder **(d)**, working toward the tail. This is the first bead in row 3. For each stitch, pick up a bead, skip a bead in the previous row, and sew through the next bead until you reach the first bead picked up

in the previous row **(e)**. The beads added in this row sit higher than the previous row and are referred to as "up-beads."
3. For each stitch in subsequent rows, pick up a bead, and sew through the next up-bead in the previous row. Continue back and forth in this manner until the band is 46 rows long.

TIP To count peyote stitch rows, add the total number of beads along both straight edges.

4. Pick up a Spike Unit, wrap the beaded band around the center of the unit where the two flat ends are glued together. "Zip up" the ends of the beaded band by matching up the end rows of the beaded band so they fit together **(f)**. "Zip up" the pieces with the working thread by zigzagging through the up-beads on both ends **(g)**.
5. Secure the band to the Spike Unit by sewing through the band and the holes in the spike beads several times. Tie a few half-hitch knots **(Basics, p. 110)**. End the threads **(Basics, p. 110)**.
6. Repeat for the remaining Spike Units.

e

Fish leather band

1. Measure your wrist and add at least 2". Trim the fish leather to this length.

2. Make a mark approximately ¾" from each end of the fish leather band. Using a leather punch, make a small hole at each mark.

3. Following the manufacturer's instructions, set the snaps in the holes.

4. On the back of the band, locate the center and measure 2½" in both directions toward the ends. Make a small mark at each point **(h)**.

Assembly

1. Attach a stop bead on a 3' length of Fireline, leaving a 12" tail **(Basics, p. 110)**. Pick up an 11º round seed bead, a melon bead, a spacer bead, and a melon bead, and sew through the center cylinder bead of a Spike Unit **(i)**.

2. Sew through the adjacent cylinder beads in the band and a hole in the spike bead. Sew through the cylinder beads on this side of the Spike Unit and exit the center bead on the opposite side of the Unit from the center cylinder in step 1. Pick up a melon bead, a spacer bead, and a melon bead, and sew through a center cylinder bead in the next Spike Unit.

3. Work as in step 2 to add the remaining Spike Units. Pick up a melon bead, a spacer bead, a melon bead, and an 11º round bead.

4. Wrap the bracelet over your wrist or another curved surface. Lay the beads across the surface and notice where the strand of beads ends on the leather. Insert the needle at this point through the leather from front to back. This should match up with a mark made in step 4 of "Fish leather band."

f

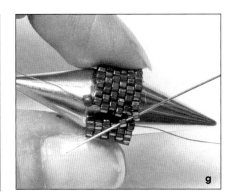

g

h

5. Make a small stitch sewing back through the fish leather, near the four beads. Continue through the center cylinder in the Spike Unit. Sew back through the melon bead, spacer, melon bead, and 11º round bead. Continue down through the fish leather from front to back. Retrace the thread path again to secure this end of the beads to the leather. End the working thread.

6. Before securing the other end of the beads to the leather, wrap the leather band around your wrist and bring the beads across the band. Thread a needle on the tail and sew down through the

i

leather from front to back where this end of the beads meet the leather. Work as in step 5 to secure this end of the beads to the leather band.

TIP When you lay the bracelet flat, the strand of beads with not lie flat. This is to accommodate the curve of your wrist when you wear the cuff. If you like, tack the strand to the fish leather by making a few stitches between the melon beads and the spacers to secure the strand.

designer NOTE

I did not trim the sides of the fish leather, preferring to leave them in their original state as I felt it added more authenticity to the bracelet.

Dragon's Claws bracelet

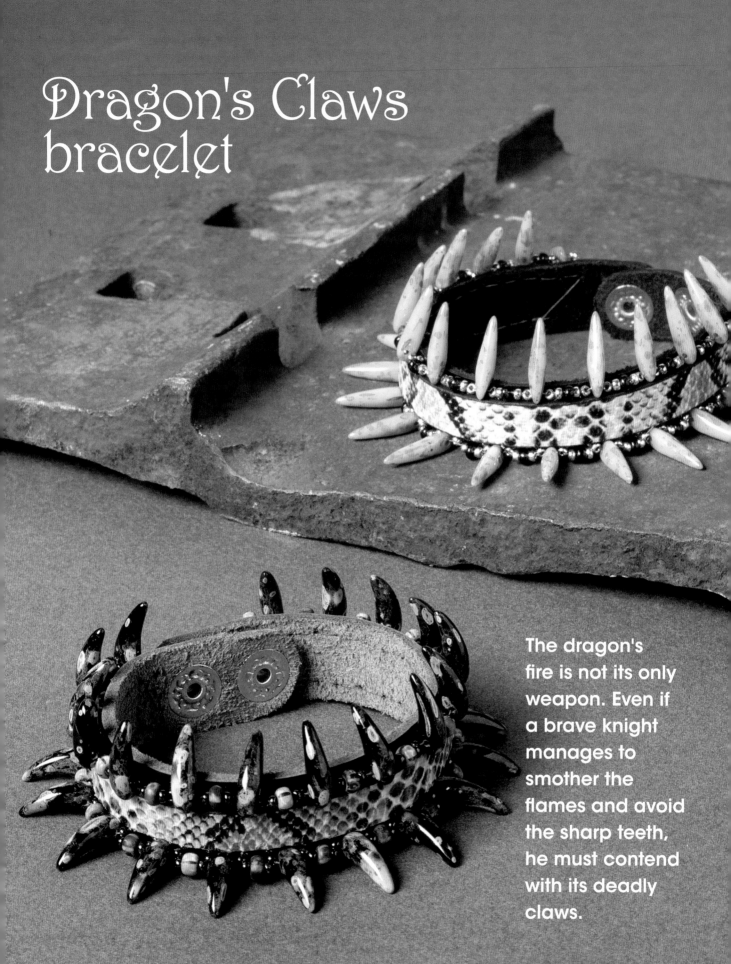

The dragon's fire is not its only weapon. Even if a brave knight manages to smother the flames and avoid the sharp teeth, he must contend with its deadly claws.

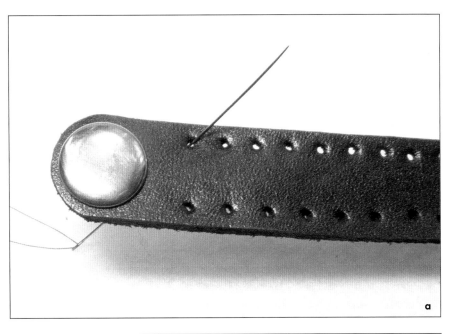

a

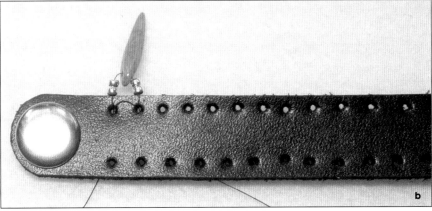

b

MATERIALS & TOOLS

- **32** 8º seed beads
- 1g 11º seed beads
- **32** 15mm glass thorn beads
- 17mm wide leather bracelet with holes
- 8mm wide decorative leather band
- Fireline 6-lb. test

⚭

- Beading needle #10
- Clamps, bulldog clips, or clothes pins
- E6000 glue
- Scissors
- Toothpick (optional)

Instructions

Beaded edging

1. Thread the needle onto 3' of Fireline. Sew up through an end hole along one edge of the leather bracelet from back to front **(a)**, leaving a 6" tail. Sew down through the next hole along this edge from front to back, and then sew back up through the first hole again from back to front.

2. Pick up two 11º seed beads, a thorn bead, and two 11ºs. Sew down through the next hole from front to back **(b)**.
3. Sew up through the next available hole in the row from back to front, and work as in step 2. Repeat this step for all remaining holes in this row. You will end on the back of the bracelet with your Fireline exiting the last hole along this edge.

4. Working back toward the tail, sew up through the next hole in the row from back to front, and continue through the two 11ºs added in step 2 **(c)**.

5. Pick up an 11º, an 8º, and an 11º. Sew down through the next two 11º beads **(d)**.

6. Sew up through the next hole and the two 11ºs. Pick up an 11º, an 8º, and an 11º. Sew down through the last two 11ºs added in the previous steps.

7. Work as in step 5 for the remainder of the row.

8. Sew up through the first hole in the row on the other side of the bracelet. Work as in steps 2–7 to embellish this edge of the leather bracelet.

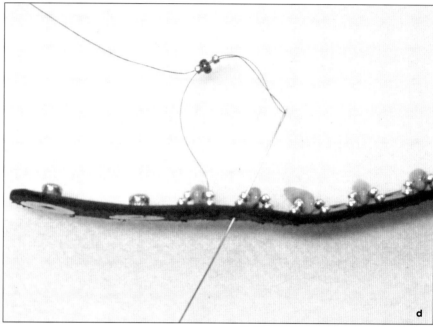

Leather strip

1. Lay the decorative leather band face down on your work surface. Apply a thin line of E6000 to the back of the strip.

2. Carefully position the decorative leather band, glue side down, along the center of the leather bracelet between the two rows of beading **(e)**.

3. Clamp the band to secure it and allow the glue to dry.

TIPS As you press the strip down, make sure you curve the bracelet, otherwise, this leather strip will buckle.

If any glue seeps out from under the leather strip, use a toothpick to clean up the excess.

Stolen Dreams bracelet

Adorned with the ornaments of far-off lands, the servant refills her master's cup. Though she is bound, they will never break her spirit or steal the untold treasures of her imagination.

- 1½" copper mandala
- **2** 4mm round jump rings, copper
- **2** 6mm round jump rings, copper
- **33** 8mm round jump rings, copper
- **24** 12mm round jump rings, copper
- **8** 4 x 4¾" oval jump rings, copper
- **5** 3mm magatama drop beads, cranberry gold cluster
- 3" small-link copper chain
- **2** 1" small-link copper chains

- Flatnose pliers
- **2** pairs chainnose pliers
- Wire cutters

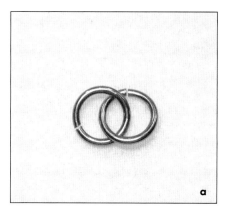

a

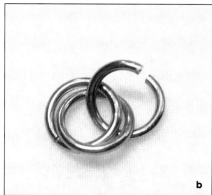

b

c

d

Instructions

Three-Ring Units

1. Open 16 12mm jump rings and close eight 12mm rings **(Basics, p. 109)**. Slide an open 12mm ring through a closed 12mm ring. Close the jump ring to form a double ring **(a)**.

2. Slide an open 12mm ring through the double ring from the previous step **(b)**, and close the ring. This completes a Three-Ring Unit.

3. Repeat steps 1 and 2 seven times for a total of eight Three-Ring Units.

Assembly

1. Open a 4mm round jump ring. Attach the bar of the toggle and a closed 4mm jump ring. Close the ring.

2. Open 17 8mm jump rings and close the remaining 16 8mm rings. (You'll have to open them wider than usual to accommodate the Three-Ring Units.)

3. Slide an open 8mm ring through the end 4mm ring and two closed 8mm rings. Close the ring **(c)**.

4. Slide an open 8mm ring through the last two 8mm rings and a Three-Ring Unit. Close the ring **(d)**.

5. Slide an open 8mm ring through the last Three-Ring Unit (added in the previous step) and two closed 8mm rings. Close the ring.

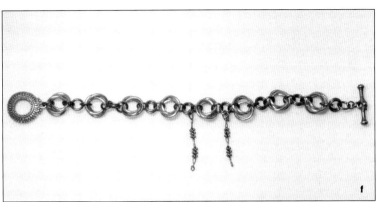

6. Repeat steps 4 and 5 six times, and then work as in step 4.

7. Slide an open 8mm ring through the last Three-Ring Unit on the bracelet and the loop of the toggle. Close the ring **(e)**.

Finger chain

1. Open a 6mm jump ring and attach the end loop of a 1" length of chain to the double 8mm rings in the bracelet fourth from one end. Close the ring. Repeat with the other 1" length of chain and the double rings that are fourth from the other end of the bracelet **(f)**.

2. Open an oval jump ring and attach the available end loop of each 1" length of chain and a hole along the outer edge of the copper mandala **(g)**. Close the ring.

3. Referring to **(h)** for position, open an oval jump ring and attach an end loop of the 3" length of chain and the hole in the mandala opposite the hole used in the previous step. Close the ring.

4. Open an oval ring and attach the available end of the 3" chain to the adjacent hole in the mandala. Close the ring.

5. Open an oval jump ring and attach a magatama drop bead to an available hole along the edge of the mandala. Close the ring. Repeat this step as desired to embellish the edges of the mandala.

Corset cuff

In many kingdoms, a prince journeys far and wide—while a princess is expected to remain in her chamber, awaiting his return. However, a daring lady might escape to follow her own quest. Fancy jewels and a restrictive gown won't do for exploring, so wear an easy corset-style cuff as you set off on your own adventure.

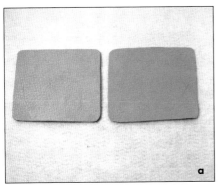

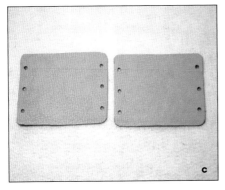

MATERIALS & TOOLS

- 6 x 2½" (7 x 6.4cm) piece of leather
- Leaf chain or other decorative beads
- **6** large jump rings
- 5mm slider bead
- **12** ⅛" (3mm) metal eyelets
- 16" 3mm leather or suede cord

∞

- Leather hole punch and eyelet setter
- **2** pairs chainnose pliers
- Sharpie marker

Instructions

Leather pieces

1. Cut two pieces of leather, each measuring 3 x 2½," and round the corners **(a)**.

2. Working on the back of one leather piece, mark the center point of the 2½" side approximately ⅛" from one edge. Also mark ¾" from the center on both sides, again placing ⅛" from the edge **(b)**. Repeat to add three marks to the other side of the leather piece, and then mark the second leather piece.

3. Using a leather hole punch, punch a ⅛" hole at each mark **(c)**.

4. Insert an eyelet into one hole from front to back. Using an eyelet setting tool, follow the manufacturer's instructions to set the eyelet **(d)**. Repeat this step for all of the remaining holes **(e)**.

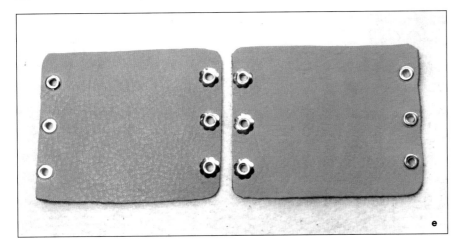

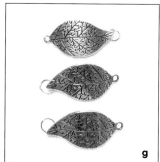

Connections

1. Select a decorative link of embellished chain like the one shown in **f**, and separate three leaves from the chain. Remove the jump ring from the stem end of each leaf **(g)**.

2. Open a large jump ring. Attach the loop at the stem end of the leaf to the top eyelet on one end of a leather piece, making sure the leaf is right side up **(h)**.

3. Repeat this process for the remaining two leaves.

4. Attach the remaining ends of the leaves to the corresponding eyelets on the second piece of leather using the technique described in steps 1–2 **(i)**.

TIP If you accidentally secure an eyelet backwards, use a small screwdriver to pry up the scrunched edges. Carefully remove the eyelet without tearing the hole. It's better to have an eyelet that is snug in the hole, than one that is loose.

Corset closure

1. Cut a 16" length of leather or suede cord and lace it through the eyelets as you would a corset or shoe lace **(j)**.

2. String a 5mm slider bead over both ends of the cord.

3. Tie both ends of the cord together with an overhand knot **(k)**. Trim the cord ends if necessary.

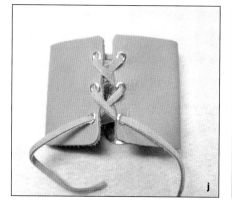

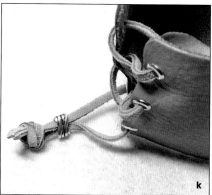

designer NOTE

This cuff is designed to fit a 7–8" wrist. If your wrist is smaller or larger, simply adjust the length of each leather piece or use a smaller bead or finding for the connection. This cuff can be worn with the corset connection side up, or with the beaded side up.

Blacksmith's Forged bracelet

Hammered links, formed in the forge by scorching flame, give strength to a knight's chainmaille armor. A blade can not pierce the sturdy mesh, unless aided by a spell, of course ...

- **3** 6mm jump rings, silver
- **124** 6mm jump rings, black
- **118** 10mm jump rings, silver
- Lobster claw clasp, silver

- Flatnose pliers
- **2** pairs chainnose pliers

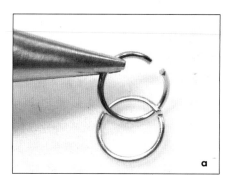

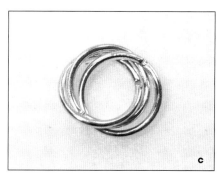

Instructions

Preparation

1. To make this project move along quicker, open 78 10mm silver jump rings and close 40 10mm silver jump rings **(Basics, p. 109)**. This makes it easier to pick up a jump ring without having to put down one pair of pliers.

2. Open all 6mm jump rings.

Three-Ring Units

1. Attach an open 10mm silver jump ring to a closed silver jump ring **(a)**. Close the jump ring.

2. Slide an open 10mm silver jump ring through the two-jump-ring segment from the previous step **(b)**. Close the ring and set the new Three-Ring Unit aside **(c)**.

3. Repeat steps 1 and 2 for a total of 39 Three-Ring Units.

Assembly

1. Slide an open 6mm black jump ring through two Three-Ring Units. Close the jump ring. Repeat this step with another open 6mm black jump ring and the same Three-Ring Unit **(d)**. This is called "doubling," and in these instructions, any time you see the words "double the ring," it means to add a second 6mm jump ring right next to the previous ring.

2. Slide an open black 6mm jump ring through one of the Three-Ring Units in the step above and a new Three-Ring Unit. Close the ring. Double the ring. This will be the first row of your bracelet. Set this row aside **(e)**.

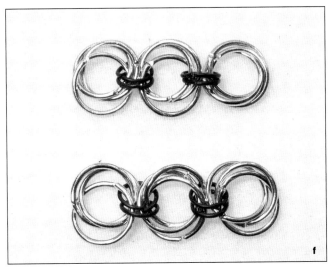

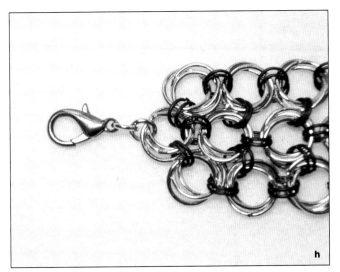

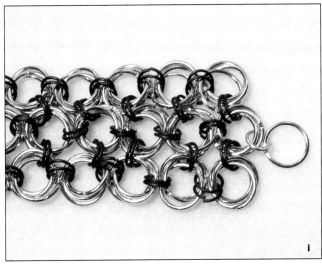

3. Work as in steps 1–2 to create a total of 13 rows.

4. To connect the rows: Position the first and second row as show **(f)**. Slide an open black 6mm jump ring through each of the end Three-Ring Units in both rows on one side. Close the jump ring. Double the ring.

5. Work as in step 4 to connect the middle rings and the other end rings in both rows **(g)**.

6. Continue working as in steps 1–6 until you have created and connected all 13 rows.

Adding the clasp

1. Attach a lobster claw clasp to a silver 6mm jump ring and close the ring. Use a silver 6mm jump ring to attach the previous silver 6mm jump ring and the center Three-Ring Unit on one end of the bracelet **(h)**.

2. On the other end of the bracelet, open a silver 6mm jump ring and attach a closed 10mm jump ring and the center Three-Ring Unit. Close the ring **(i)**.

Tribal Queen's Gauntlet bracelet

With her power and grace, she has conquered kingdoms and captured the respect of her people. She moves ahead with unstoppable determination to fulfill that which is her destiny.

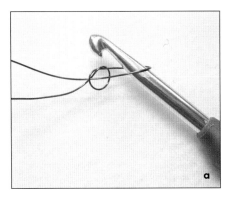

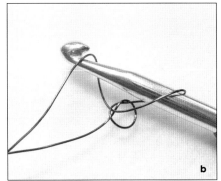

MATERIALS & TOOLS

- **33–45** 4x20mm metal drops on chain, gunmetal
- **6** 22mm fancy-ribbon crimps, bronze
- 150' spool 24-gauge Parawire, bronze
- **6** 6mm split ring, bronze
- **3** lobster claw clasps

- **2** pairs chainnose pliers
- Flatnose pliers
- Metal crochet hook size I (5.50mm)
- Roundnose pliers
- Split ring pliers
- Wire cutters

Instructions

Band

1. Leaving the 24-gauge wire on the spool, make a slip knot **(Basics, p. 110)** leaving a 2" tail. Insert the crochet hook into the loop **(a)**.

2. Row 1: Work a chain stitch by loosely wrapping the wire over the hook **(b)** and pulling the wire through the loop **(Basics p. 110) (c)**. Repeat this stitch 11 times. This completes the first row **(d)**.

3. Row 2: Working toward the tail, work a row of single crochet by inserting the hook into the top loop of the previous stitch **(Basics, p. 110) (e)**. Wrap the wire over

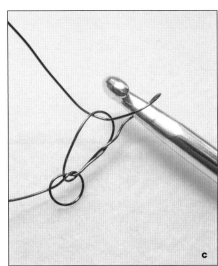

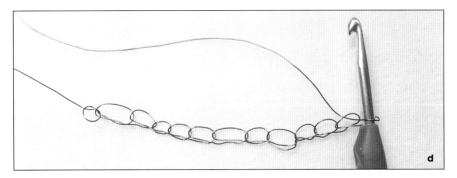

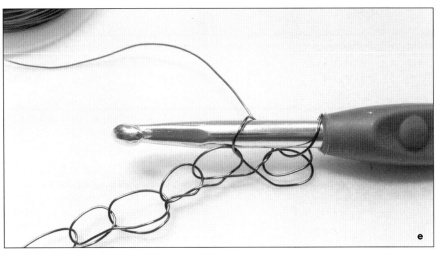

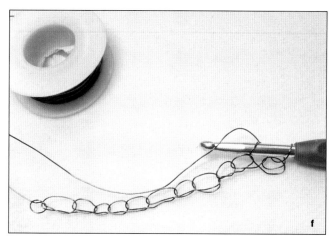

f

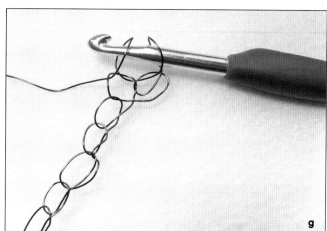

g

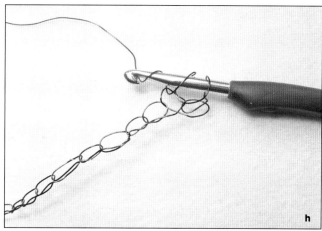

h

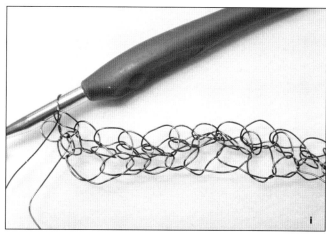

i

j

k

the hook **(f)**, and pull the wire through the loop. There are now two loops on the hook **(g)**. Wrap the wire over the hook **(h)** and pull the hook through both loops. Repeat this 10 times, and then work one chain stitch as in step 2 to complete the second row **(i)**. Using your fingers, gently bend the front loops in the second row up, and turn your work to be in position for the next row.

4. For all remaining rows: Work as in Step 3 until you have a band that will fit comfortably around your wrist and forearm. Trim the wire, leaving a 1" tail.

Charms

1. Using two pairs of pliers, remove the metal drops from the chain by opening each jump ring **(Basics, p. 109)** and sliding them off the chain **(j)**.

2. Identify the center row of crochet on the band, and insert the jump ring and the drop through the wire in the center row **(k)** and close the jump ring **(l)**.

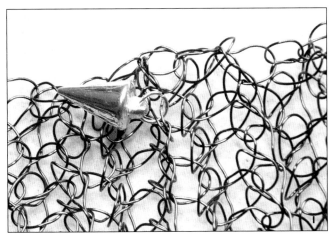

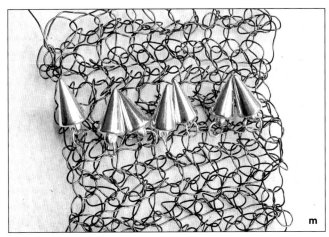

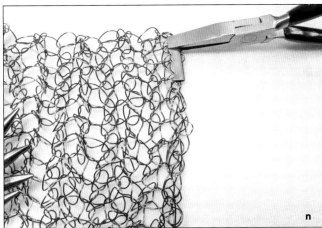

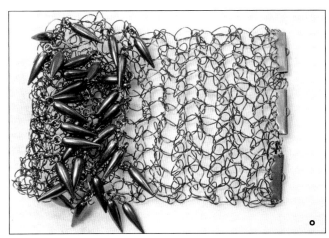

Repeat to add 10 or 11 drops to the center row **(m)**.

3. Work as in step 2 for each row of the band on either side of the center row.

Closure

1. On one end of the band, weave the end wire back and forth through the last row in the band and press it down with flatnose pliers **(Basics, p. 110)**. Repeat on the other end with the tail.

2. On one end of the band, place a fancy ribbon crimp over the end near the short edge **(n)** and crimp it with flatnose pliers. Repeat to add two more ribbon crimps to this end of the band **(o)**.

3. Work as in step 2 to add three crimps to the other end of the band.

4. Using split ring pliers, open a split ring and attach it to the loop of a ribbon crimp **(p)**. Repeat with the remaining five crimps and split rings.

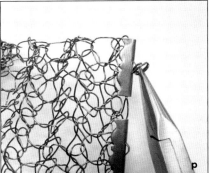

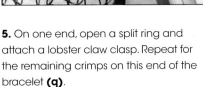

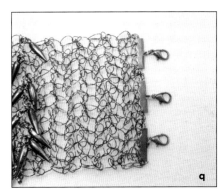

5. On one end, open a split ring and attach a lobster claw clasp. Repeat for the remaining crimps on this end of the bracelet **(q)**.

TIP This bracelet can be tricky to put on by yourself. However, the wire is a bit stretchy so rather than unclasp the cuff, I make sure the clasps are secure first, and then carefully slide it over my hand and wrist.

Hobnail wrist wrap

Protection comes in many forms. Humble hobnails (short nails with large heads) are essential for boots that can withstand sharp cobblestones—or the scaly hide of an angry dragon.

a

b

Instructions

1. Position a domed stud on the block and carefully hammer the top surface of the stud **(a)**. Repeat for as many or as few of the studs as you desire. Set aside.

2. Wrap the bracelet around your wrist and secure the peg closure into position so the bracelet fits as desired. Remove the bracelet and wrap it again (off of your wrist) **(b)**. Mark the back of each wrap directly across from the peg. You are identifying where the hobnails will sit on the top of your wrist when the bracelet is worn.

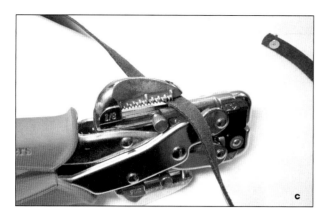

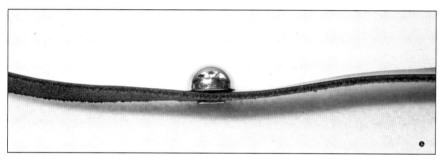

3. With a leather hole punch, punch a ⅛" hole at each of the marks made in the previous step **(c)**.

4. Randomly make one or two punches on either side of the mark on each wrap. Don't be afraid to punch some of the holes slightly off center of the band.

5. Insert the screw from back to front through a hole in the band **(d)**. Screw the domed stud onto the post **(e)**. Repeat for the remaining holes. The off-center holes will add to the rustic look **(f)**.

Earrings

Trembling Scales earrings

Floating and fluttering like strands of moss on a hoary castle wall, tiny scales from a captured dragon hang in beautiful disarray, shuddering with each wild wind that blows through the courtyard.

- **10** Czech glass dragon scale beads, silver
- **2** 5mm bicone crystals, red
- 22-gauge Artistic wire, silver
- 28-gauge Artistic wire, silver
- **2** French hook earring wires, silver
- **2** swirl hooks, silver (www.greengirlstudios com)

- Chainnose pliers
- Roundnose pliers
- Wire cutters

Instructions

1. On a 4" length of 22-gauge Artistic wire, attach a swirl hook as you would a top-drilled bead **(Basics, p. 108)**, leaving a 1" tail. Wrap the tail around the working wire approximately 2–3mm above the swirl. Make several wraps and trim the tail **(a)**.

2. String a 4mm bicone crystal onto the wire and make the first half of a wrapped loop above the crystal. Slide the loop of an earring wire onto the wire, and complete the wraps **(Basics, p. 108)**. Trim the wire **(b)**.

3. Using wire cutters, cut a 16" length of 28-gauge wire, and make a few wraps along the bottom of the swirl to secure the wire **(c)**.

4. String a glass dragon scale bead onto the wire and make a wrap. Gently pull on the dragon scale to make sure there is just enough slack in the wire so the scale can move freely. Make two or three tight wraps around the swirl **(d)**. Repeat with four more dragon scales; trim the wire and tuck the end under the wrapped wire. Use chainnose pliers to adjust the wraps and the position of the dragon scales, if necessary.

5. Repeat steps 1–4 to make a second earring, paying attention to the direction of the swirl when you attach the earring wire so it is a mirror image of the first earring.

Orb of the Raven earrings

The future is murky for
mere mortals, but one
glimpse into the raven's
orb reveals all. Face
your fate, if you dare ...

Instructions

Up-and-Down earring wire

1. Using roundnose pliers, make a plain loop **(Basics, p. 108)** on one end of a 3" length of 22-gauge Artistic wire **(a)**.

2. Using chainnose pliers, make a 90-degree bend in the wire just above the plain loop **(b)**.

3. String a 4mm round crystal (shown as a blue bead for example purposes) onto the wire and push the crystal down to sit above the plain loop.

4. Using flatnose pliers, grasp the wire approximately 1¾" above the last bend created in step **2**. Make a bend so the tail is now pointing down **(c)**.

5. With your fingers, gently form the wire so it curves into an almond shape **(d)**.

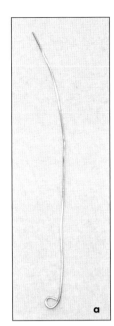
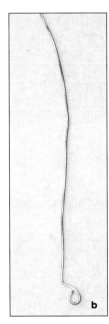

- **6** 4mm round crystals, clear
- **2** claw and globe charms with jump rings, silver
- **2** 3" lengths of 22-gauge Artistic wire, silver
- **2** 4" lengths of small-link chain, silver
- **4** 2" head pins, silver

- Cup bur
- **2** pairs chainnose pliers
- **2** pairs flatnose pliers
- Roundnose pliers
- Wire cutters

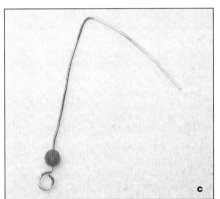

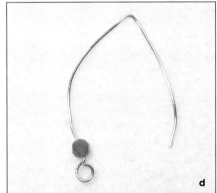

6. Trim the tail as needed, and file the end smooth using a cup bur.

7. Make a second earring wire **(Basics, p. 109)**.

Dangles

1. String a 4mm round crystal onto a head pin and, using roundnose pliers, make a plain loop **(e)**. Repeat to make a total of four crystal dangles.

2. On each end of a 4" length of chain, open the loop of a dangle and attach it to an end link **(Basics, p. 109) (f)**. Repeat to attach a dangle to each end of the remaining length of chain.

Assembly

1. Open the jump ring on the claw and globe charm. Attach the loop of the earring wire to a link in the chain that is 1½" from one end of the chain. Close the jump ring **(Basics, p. 109) (g)**.

2. Repeat for the second earring.

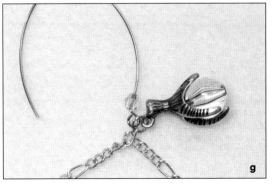

Lady-in-Waiting earrings

Even the Queen's servants bedeck themselves in finery. The ladies of the court who live in the castle and attend Her Majesty still vie for the eye of a handsome suitor.

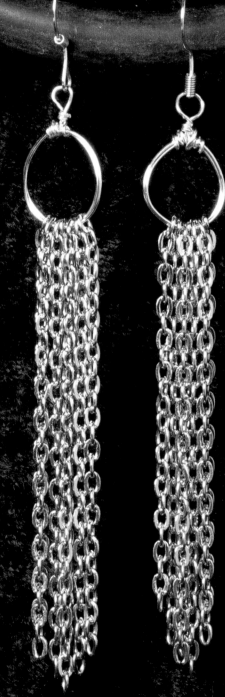

MATERIALS & TOOLS

- 5mm link chain or other small- link chain, silver
- 16" 24-gauge Artistic wire, silver
- **2** earring wires, silver

- **2** pairs chainnose pliers
- Roundnose pliers
- Wire cutters

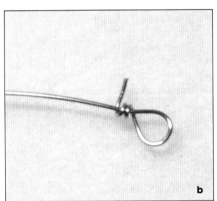

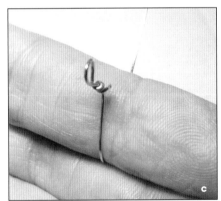

Instructions

1. Cut 14 pieces of chain, varying between 2½" and 2¾" in length. Arrange seven lengths of the chain on your work surface so the center chain is the longest chain in the group **(a)**.

2. Cut two 8" lengths of 24-gauge Artistic wire.

3. On one end of a piece of wire, make a wrapped loop **(Basics, p. 108)** using roundnose pliers **(b)**.

4. Position the wire on your finger so the wrapped loop is in the center of your finger **(c)**.

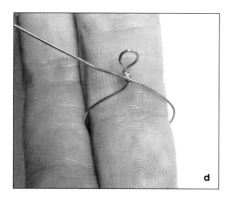

5. Loosely wrap the wire around your finger **(d)** two times. Remove the wire from your finger.

6. String an end link of each chain on the wire, making sure the longest chain is in the center **(e)**.

7. Carefully guide the wire through the end link of the chains again **(f)**.

8. Bring the end of the wire slightly past the wrapped loop made in step 1, and adjust the wire loops to the desired size.

9. Wrap the wire around both loops of wire next to the wrapped loop **(g)**.

10. Bring the wire to the other side of the wrapped loop and make a few wraps.

11. Wrap the wire once or twice around the base of the wrapped loop. Trim the wire and press the end to the wirework.

12. Open the loop of an earring wire and attach it to the wrapped loop. Close the loop **(Basics, p. 109)**.

13. Make a second earring.

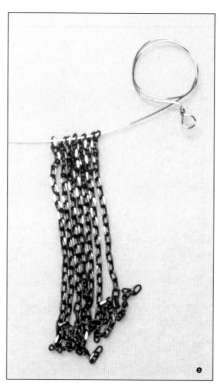

Amethyst Alchemy earrings

Sorcerers and silversmiths labor to master the art of capturing gems in precious metal. The end result, whether by spell or by skill, is a truly magical transformation.

a

b

c

back view

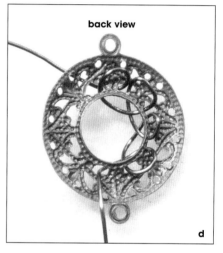

d

Instructions

Rivoli ring connector

1. Cut an 11" length of 24-gauge Parawire. Insert one end through a hole along the inner edge of the ring connector from front to back. Center the connector on the wire. Bring the wire through the next hole along the inner edge of the connector from back to front. Snug up the wire **(a)**.

2. Continue working with the same end of the wire, using a pair of chainnose pliers, if necessary, to guide and snug the wire. Insert the wire from front to back through the hole to the left of the first hole **(b)**, and up through the same hole the other end of the wire is exiting. Snug up the wire slightly to form a small loop.

3. Working counter clockwise, skip the next hole along the inner edge. Insert the working end down through the next hole from front to back, up through the previous hole, and snug up the wire slightly. Continue in this manner until you reach the inner hole opposite the one you started with in step 1 **(c)**. Make sure the wire is snug on the back of the connector **(d)**.

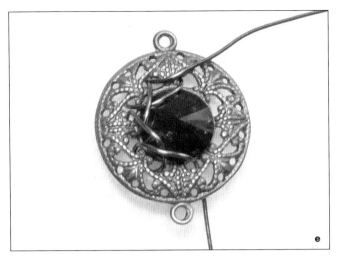

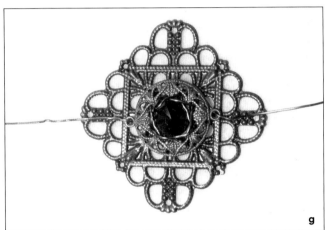

back view

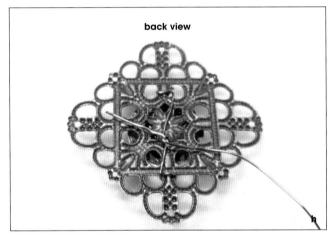

4. Position the Rivoli in the center of the connector with the lip of the Rivoli under the wire loops created in steps 2–4.

TIP In order not to scratch the Rivoli, use a pair of chainnose pliers to loosen the loops, if necessary.

5. Holding the Rivoli in place with your thumb and working clockwise with the other end of the wire, weave the wire through the inner holes as you did for the first side of the wire **(e)**. Use a firm tension to secure the rivoli to the center of the connector. Make sure both wires end at the back of the component.

6. With one end of the wire, go up through an end loop of the ring connector. Repeat with the other end of the wire and the available loop of the ring connector **(f)**.

7. Make a second Rivoli ring connector.

Assembly

1. Center a Rivoli ring connector on a 36mm filigree square, making sure each end loop of the connector aligns with an outer corner of the square **(g)**. Insert one end of the wire through the filigree square from front to back. Repeat with the other end, and twist the two ends together a few times on the back of the filigree square to tighten **(h)**.

2. Insert one end of the wire up to the front of the square and back down through an adjacent hole. Make sure this step is hidden behind the Rivoli ring connector. Repeat with the other end of the wire. Trim the wires and tuck the ends.

3. Open the loop of an earring wire. Attach one corner of the filigree square to the earring wire and close the loop **(Basics, p. 109)**.

4. Make a second earring.

Dragon's Gold earrings

Hidden away in a secret cave, the dragon's treasure trove awaits. Only the bravest and cleverest warrior will defeat the guardian of the gold and steal its prize.

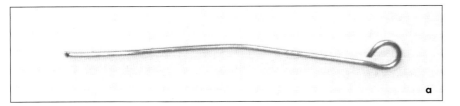

a

b

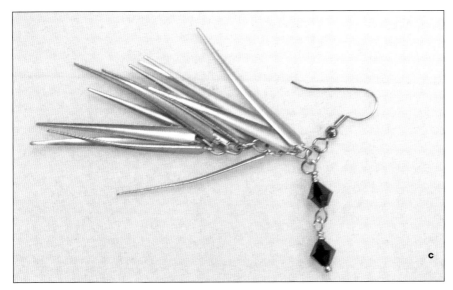

c

MATERIALS & TOOLS

- **4** 6mm bicone crystals, red
- **2** 3mm daisy spacer beads or 11º seed beads, gold
- **2** long dagger chain pendants, matte gold
- 3" 22-gauge Artistic wire, gold
- **2** 1" head pins, gold
- **2** earring wires (optional instructions to make your own are included)

- **2** pairs chainnose pliers
- Roundnose pliers
- Wire cutters

Instructions

Bicone dangle component

1. Cut a 1½" length of 22-gauge wire. On one end, use roundnose pliers to make a plain loop **(Basics, p. 108) (a)**.

2. Pick up a 6mm bicone crystal, and make a wrapped loop **(Basics, p. 108)**.

3. On a head pin, string a 3mm daisy spacer (or 11º seed bead) and a crystal. Make the first half of a wrapped loop.

Attach it to the plain loop of the dangle created in step 1, and complete the wraps **(b)**.

4. Repeat steps 1–3 to make a second crystal dangle component.

Assembly

1. Open the top link of a dagger chain pendant and attach it to the loop of a bicone dangle component and the loop of an earring wire. Close the link **(c)**.

2. Repeat to make a second earring.

designer NOTE

Why not make your own earring wires? It's easy, inexpensive, and allows for even more creativity in your jewelry!
See **Basics, p. 109** for complete, step-by-step instructions.

Serpent's Scales earrings

Harness the hypnotic power of the serpent. The perfect mix of beauty and danger, its undulating form is impossible to resist — but its poisonous fangs mean instant death.

a

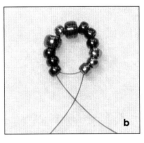

b

c

d

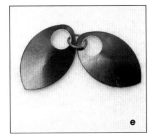

e

f

g

MATERIALS & TOOLS

- **2** 8º hex cut seed beads
- **4** 8º seed beads
- 1g 11º seed beads, color A
- 1g 11º seed beads, color B
- **8** 14x22mm aluminum scales color A (black)
- **4** 14x22mm aluminum scales color B (red)
- **6** 5mm jump rings, bronze
- **2** earring wires
- Fireline 6-lb. test

- Beading needle #10
- Flatnose pliers
- **2** pairs chainnose pliers
- Scissors

Instructions

Beaded embellishment

1. Thread a needle with an 8" length of Fireline, pick up three color A 11º seed beads, three color B 11º seed beads, an 8º seed bead, an A, an 8º, and three Bs **(a)**. Sew through all the beads again to form a ring **(b)**. Continue through the next eight beads to exit the A between the two 8ºs **(c)**.

2. Pick up an A, an 8º hex-cut seed bead, and an A, and sew through the A that your thread was exiting at the start of this step **(d)**. Retrace the thread path. Continue through the nearest six beads in the original ring, making a couple of half-hitch knots **(Basics, p. 110)**. End the threads **(Basics, p. 110)**.

3. Make a second beaded embellishment.

Scale dangle

1. Using two pairs of chainnose pliers, open three 5mm jump rings **(Basics, p. 109)**.

2. On one jump ring, pick up a small black scale from front to back, and another black scale from back to front. Close the jump ring **(e)**. You have completed the first scale unit.

3. On a jump ring, pick up a small red scale from front to back, the jump ring in the first scale unit, and a red scale from back to front. Close the jump ring **(f)**.

4. Work as in step 3 with a pair of black scales, but adding a beaded embellishment before you pick up the first scale. Pick up the loop of an earring wire after you pick up the second scale. Close the jump ring **(g)**.

5. Make a second earring.

Tethys earrings

Tethys is the pagan goddess of fresh water and the mother of rivers and streams. If you look closely, you may see mermaids splashing within her shimmering waterfalls and deep pools.

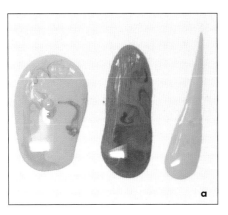

a

b

c

Instructions

Painting the components

1. Cover your work surface with a layer of paper towels and place a chandelier component face up on the paper towel.
2. With the lid secure, shake each metal paint vigorously to activate the metal ball and mix the paint.
3. Squeeze a modest amount of each color of paint onto the paper plate **(a)**.
4. Apply the paint lightly to the component with a foam brush or paint brush **(b)**. Repeat for the remaining components, including the stamped tubes and jump rings.
5. Allow the paint to dry for a few minutes and then turn the components over and paint the back **(c)**.
6. Optional Step: If you desire more of an aged look to your chandelier components, or if the paint is too thick in one area and you cannot see the definition of the metal, apply a small amount of nail polish remover to a cotton swab, and gently dab the component to remove the excess paint. **Photo d** shows the before image and **photo e** shows the component after some of the paint has been removed.
7. Using the nail polish remover and a cotton swab, gently remove the paint from the stamped tubes, except in the recessed areas.

TIP If you remove too much paint, work as in steps 3 and 4, adding and removing paint until you achieve the desired effect.

MATERIALS & TOOLS

- **4** 22mm chandelier earring components
- **10** 3x14mm stamped metal tubes
- **8** 3mm magatama drops, lavender storm gold luster iris
- **8** 4mm jump rings, silver
- **2** 6mm jump rings, silver
- **10** 1½" head pins, silver
- **2** earring wires
- Glaze gloss metal sealer
- Nail polish remover *(optional)*
- 3 colors of patina metal paint
  - Jade
  - Moss
  - Verdigris

- **2** pairs chainnose or flatnose pliers
- Cotton swab *(or make-up pads)*
- Foam brush *(or paint brush)*
- Paper towels
- Roundnose pliers
- Small paper plate
- Wire cutters

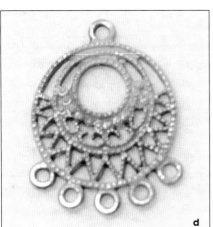

d

e

f

g

h

i

j

8. Squeeze a generous amount of glaze onto a paper plate, and apply a thin layer to the components with clean brush.

9. Once the components are dry and the glaze has set, open a 6mm jump ring **(Basics, p. 109)** and use it to attach the center loop of the five loops along the lower edge of a chandelier component. (we will call this the "top component") and the top loop of another chandelier component (this is called the "bottom component"). Close the jump ring **(f)**.

10. On a 1½" head pin, string a stamped tube **(g)**. Using roundnose pliers, make the first half of a wrapped loop

k

l

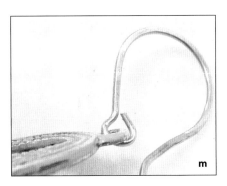

m

(Basics, p. 108) (h). Attach the loop to an available loop on a bottom component (i) and complete the wraps (j). Repeat for the remaining available loops along the lower edge on the bottom component (k).

11. Open a 4mm jump ring. Attach a 3mm magatama drop bead to an available loop along the lower edge of the top component. Close the jump ring (l). Repeat this step for the remaining loops along the lower edge of the top component.

12. Open the loop of an earring wire and attach it to the loop at the top of the top component. Close the loop (m).

13. Repeat to make a second earring.

designer NOTES

I love long earrings, but some times they can be too heavy. To lighten the load, I simply embellish a single chandelier component for each earring with magatama drop beads and attach a long earring wire (right).

If you prefer a shorter, lighter earring, make the earrings as described above, but attach a traditional French earring wire, in place of the long wire (below).

Chainmaille Bellflower earrings

A nosegay in the spring is a tender mark of affection from a knight to his lady. No jeweled crown can compare with the sweet blossoms from her one, true love.

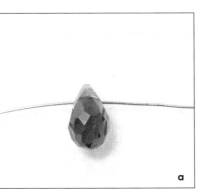

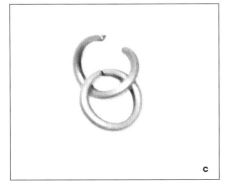

MATERIALS & TOOLS

- **34** 6mm heavy-gauge jump rings, copper
- **4** 8mm heavy-gauge jump rings, copper
- **2** 6 x 12mm top-drilled crystal briolette
- 6" 24-gauge wire, copper

- **2** pairs chainnose pliers
- Wire cutters

Instructions

Dangle

1. Cut a 3" length of 24-gauge wire. Center a 6x12mm briolette on the wire **(a)**.

2. Pull the ends of the wire up so they cross each other above the briolette **(b)**. Make wraps above the bead **(Basics, p. 108)**.

3. With the remaining wire, use roundnose pliers to make a wrapped loop **(Basics, p. 108)**, and trim the wires. Repeat to make second earring.

Assembly

1. Open twelve 6mm jump rings and close five 6 mm jump rings. Open one 8mm jump ring and close one 8mm jump ring. Attach a closed 6mm jump ring to an open 6mm jump ring **(Basics, p. 108) (c).** Close the jump ring **(d).** Repeat for a total of five Two-Ring Units.

e

f

g

2. Slide an open 6mm jump ring through the center of a Two-Ring Unit created in step 1 **(e)**. Close the jump ring. Repeat for a total of five Two-Ring Units.

3. Use one 8mm jump ring to connect all five of the single jump rings added in the previous step and a closed 8mm jump ring **(f)**. Close the jump ring.

4. Locate the center Two-Ring Unit added in the previous step. Use one open 6mm jump ring to attach the Two-Ring Unit **(g)** and the loop of the dangle. Close the jump ring **(h)**.

5. Use an open 6mm jump ring to attach the second 8mm jump ring added in step 3 and the loop of an earring wire. Close the jump ring **(i)**.

6. Repeat assembly steps 1–5 to make a second earrings.

h

i

Basics

Materials

Beading threads

Accuflex

Beadalon beading wire

Fireline

Wire

twisted wire

Parawire

Artistic wire

Cords

leather

suede

satin/silk

Leather

strip

fish leather

bracelet w/snaps

wrap bracelet

Chain

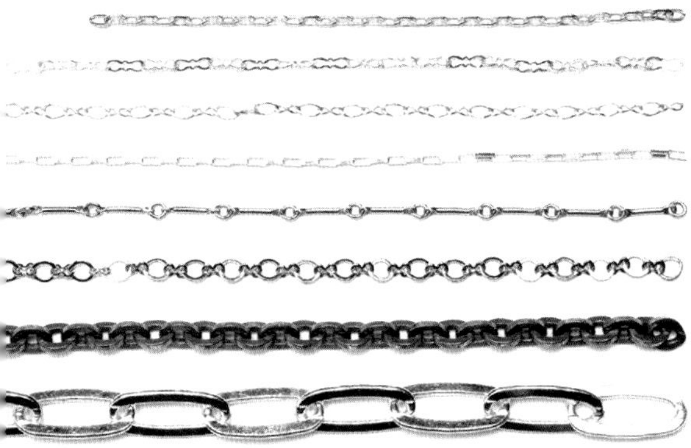

assorted

metal drop

extender

Metal Findings

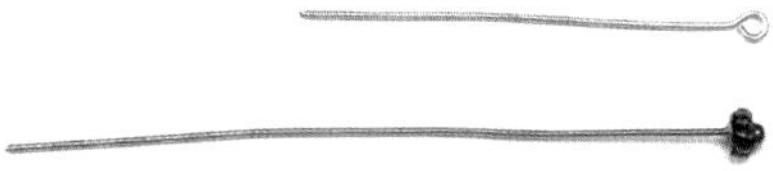

head pins

ribbon crimps

crimp beads

crimp covers

round jump rings

oval jump rings

split rings

end cones

domed screw-back studs

bead caps

aluminum scales

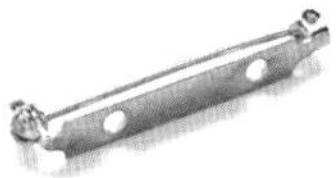

bar pin back

Clasps

S-hook

toggle

lobster claw

Earring Findings

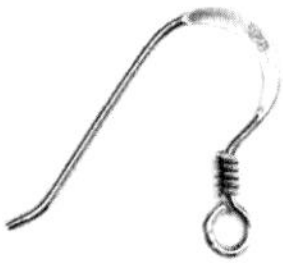

French hooks

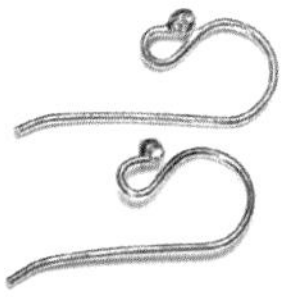

earring wires

chandelier earrings

Beads

bicone crystal

round crystal

briolette

spike beads

seed beads

crystal sticks

hex cut beads

spacers

fire-polished

wooden beehive

wooden barrel

Rivolis

shell disks

glass thorn

lentil beads

magatama drops

Other

wooden laser-cut
disks

ring blanks

filigree components

metal cuff

cabachons

wire frame tiara

patina paint

gloss glaze

2-part epoxy resin

Tools

▲ Diagonal **wire cutters** are used to trim flexible beading wire and thin gauges of wire. These cutters trim the wire at an angle, leaving a point at the tip of the wire.

▲ **Chainnose pliers** have flat jaws and are used to bend and shape wire and open and close jump rings.

▲ **Flatnose** pliers have the same smooth inner jaws as chainnose pliers. They can grasp wire or components without leaving marks. The flat-shaped jaws allow for a comfortable grip in narrow or awkward spaces.

▲ **Crimping pliers** are used with crimp beads and flexible beading wire. They are used to hold and compress tube crimps into narrow cylinders that hold strung projects in place.

▲ **Roundnose pliers** have round jaws that taper to a point. They are used to shape wire and form loops.

▲ **Split-ring pliers** make it easy to open split rings. The bent tip slides between the layers of the ring, holding them apart as you add components.

▲ A **metal punch** is a hardened steel tool used to make a hole in metal.

▲ A **Leather hole punch** is an easy-to-use rotary punch that makes six different hole sizes (2mm, 2.5mm, 3mm, 3.5mm, 4mm, and 4.5mm) and works great on leather. Punch sizes are clearly labeled.

▲ **Bench blocks** are solid, smooth work surfaces, usually made of steel, that can be used for hammering and shaping metal and wire.

▲ A **kumihimo disk** is a lightweight tool used in kumihimo braiding to ensure patterns are consistent. The round shape features small divets along the edge, numbered 1 through 32, to help you follow along with patterns.

◄ A **Snap set and setting tool** can be purchased in a package, giving you everything you need to apply snaps to leather or canvas projects, including belts, bags, and cases.

▲ A **cup bur** is perfect for rounding wire ends. After the ends of wire are cut with a pair of wire cutters, the edges are often sharp. If you are making earring wires, you'll need to smooth the end of the wire that passes through the ear.

▲ A **chasing hammer** has a large, flat or slightly rounded face for flattening metal or wire. The peen side is for riveting, metal forming and texturing.

▲ **Beading needles** are similar to sewing needles, except the eye of a beading needle is almost as narrow as the shaft. The needles are numbered, and are most frequently found in sizes #10–#16. The thinner the needle, the higher the needle number.

◄ **Metal files** come in all shapes and sizes, and in all degrees of coarseness and smoothness for sanding rough edges of metal components.

▲ **Awls** are pointed tools used to pierce solid materials (such as leather) and to place or pick apart knots.

Techniques

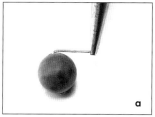   

Making a plain loop ▲

1. Trim the wire or head pin ⅜" above the bead. Make a right-angle bend close to the bead **(a)**.

2. Grab the wire's tip with roundnose pliers. The tip of the wire should be flush with the pliers. Roll the wire to form a half circle. Release the wire **(b)**.

3. Reposition the pliers in the loop and continue rolling **(c)**.

4. The finished loop should form a centered circle above the bead **(d)**.

 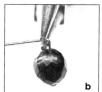    

Making a wrapped loop ▲

1. Make sure you have at least 1¼" of wire above the bead. With the tip of your chainnose pliers, grasp the wire directly above the bead. Bend the wire (above the pliers) into a right angle **(a)**.

2. Using roundnose pliers, position the jaws in the bend **(b)**.

3. Bring the wire over the top jaw of the pliers **(c)**.

4. Reposition the plier's lower jaw snugly into the loop. Curve the wire downward around the bottom of the pliers. This is the first half of a wrapped loop **(d)**.

5. Position the chainnose pliers' jaws across the loop **(e)**.

6. Wrap the wire around the wire stem, covering the stem between the loop and the top bead. Trim the excess wire and press the cut end close to the wraps with chainnose pliers **(f)**.

Making wraps above a top-drilled bead ▲

1. Center a top-drilled bead on a 3" piece of wire. Bend each end upward and cross the wires into an "X" above the bead **(a)**.

2. Using chainnose pliers, make a small bend in each wire so the ends form a right angle **(b)**.

3. Wrap the horizontal wire around the vertical wire as in a wrapped loop. Trim the wrapping wire **(c)**.

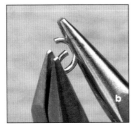

◄ Opening and closing loops or jump rings

1. Hold the loop or jump ring with two pairs of chainnose pliers **(a)**.
2. To open the loop or jump ring, bring one pair of pliers toward you and push the other pair away. String materials on the open loop or jump ring. Reverse the steps to close the open loop or jump ring **(b)**.

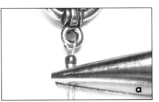

Opening a split ring ▲

Slide the hooked tip of split-ring pliers between the two overlapping wires.

Flattened crimp ▲

1. Hold the crimp using the tip of your chainnose pliers. Squeeze the pliers firmly to flatten the crimp **(a)**.
2. Pull one end of the wire to make sure the crimp has a solid grip. If the wire slides, repeat the steps with a new crimp **(b)**.

Closing a crimp cover ▲

Place the notch at the tip of the jaws of the crimping pliers around the crimp cover and squeeze gently until the two side close together.

Folded a crimp ▲

1. Position the crimp bead in the notch closest to the crimping plier's handle **(a)**.
2. Separate the wires and firmly squeeze the crimp **(b)**.

3. Move the crimp into the notch at the plier's tip and hold the crimp as shown. Squeeze the crimp bead, folding it in half at the indentation **(c)**.
4. Pull one end of the wire to test that the folded crimp is secure **(d)**.

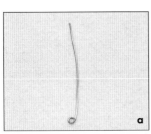

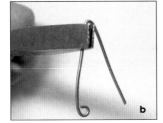

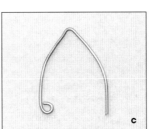

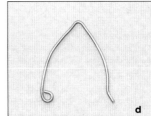

Up-and-down earring wires ▲

1. Using roundnose pliers, make a plain loop **(Basics, p. 108)** on one end of a 3" length of 22-gauge Artistic wire **(a)**.
2. Using flatnose pliers, make a 90-degree bend in the wire just above the plain loop **(b)**.

3. Using flatnose pliers, grasp the wire approximately 1¾" above the bend created in step 2, and make a bend so the tail is now pointing down **(c)**.
4. With your fingers, gently form the wire so it curves into sort of an almond shape. Bend the end outward, slightly **(d)**.
5. Trim the tail as needed and file the end smooth using a cup bur.
6. Make a second earring wire.

Ending and adding thread

To end a thread, sew back through the last few rows or rounds of beadwork, following the thread path of the stitch and tying two or three half-hitch knots (see "Half-hitch knot" below) between beads as you go. Sew through a few beads after the last knot, and trim the thread.

To add a thread, sew into the beadwork several rows or rounds prior to the point where the last bead was added, leaving a short tail. Follow the thread path of the stitch, tying a few half-hitch knots between beads as you go, and exit where the last stitch ended. Trim the short tail.

◀ Stop bead

Use a stop bead to secure beads temporarily when you begin stitching. Choose a bead that is different from the beads in your project. Pick up the stop bead, leaving the desired length tail. Sew through the stop bead again in the same direction, making sure you don't split the thread. If desired, sew through it one more time for added security.

Half-hitch knot ▲
Pass the needle under the thread bridge between two beads, and pull gently until a loop forms. Sew through the loop, and pull gently to draw the knot into the beadwork.

Overhand knot ▲
Make a loop with the thread. Pull the tail through the loop and tighten.

Square knot ▲
1. Cross one end of the thread over and under the other end. Pull both ends to tighten the first half of the knot.
2 Cross the first end of the thread over and under the other end. Pull both ends to tighten the knot.

Slip knot and chain stitch ▲
1. Leaving the desired length tail, make a loop in the cord, crossing the spool end over the tail. Insert the crochet hook through the loop, yarn over, and pull the cord through the loop.
2 Yarn over the hook, and draw through the loop. Repeat for the desired number of chain stitches.

Single crochet ▲
Insert the hook through the front and back loops of the next stitch. Yarn over, and draw through the stitch. Yarn over, and draw through remaining loops.

Acknowledgments

I'd like to thank my family for their incredible patience as I holed myself up in my bead room for months. Thanks to my daughter Sophia for her input on the projects herein. Her interest in and knowledge of mythology and "magic" proved very valuable. And thanks to my husband Anthony for being able to just close the door on the horrible mess in that room and patiently wait until I finished the book so I could clean the room!

Thanks to Dianne Wheeler, my editor, who brought me the idea for this book and for her coaching and encouragement along the way.

Thank you to Bill and Lisa for the photography and art direction for this book. I appreciate your hard work.

About the Author

Jane Danley Cruz has been making jewelry for more than 30 years. She has been designing original jewelry projects, writing instructions, and teaching classes since 1998. In 2005, she decided to forsake all other crafts, (photography, pottery, painting, knitting, crocheting, and sewing) to focus primarily on beading. For five years, she studied various jewelry-making techniques.

In 2010, Jane began working at *Bead&Button* magazine. For the next four years, she was an Associate Editor for both *Bead&Button* and *Wirework*. During 2013, she also worked as a contributing editor to *BeadStyle* magazine. In addition, she was the technical editor for a number of jewelry books published by Kalmbach Books.

When she is not making jewelry or writing instructions, Jane is thinking about jewelry, talking about jewelry, or sketching her next jewelry project.

Discover More Chain Mail Projects

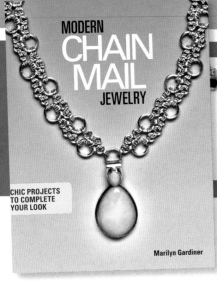

Modern Chain Mail Jewelry
Transform traditional chain mail weaves into eye-catching, wearable necklaces.

#67853 • $21.99

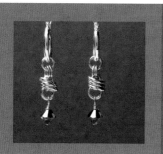

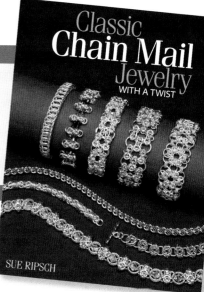

Classic Chain Mail Jewelry with a Twist
Create 30+ beautiful jewelry projects with timeless chain mail weaves.

#64834 • $21.95

Chain Mail Elegance
Use crystals and other sparkly elements to create 30 chain mail pieces that shine!

#67038 • $21.99

KALMBACH BOOKS

Buy now from your favorite craft or bead shop!
Shop at JewelryandBeadingStore.com

Sales tax where applicable.

P29558